PERGAMON GENERAL PSYCHOLOGY SERIES

Editors: Arnold P. Goldstein, *Syracuse University*
Leonard Krasner, *SUNY, Stony Brook*

THE

STRUCTURAL APPROACH

IN

PSYCHOLOGICAL TESTING

PGPS-4

THE

STRUCTURAL APPROACH

IN

PSYCHOLOGICAL TESTING

by

Marvin L. Kaplan
Nick J. Colarelli
Ruth Brill Gross
Donald Leventhal
Saul M. Siegel

PERGAMON PRESS
New York • Toronto • Oxford
Sydney • Braunschweig

Pergamon Press Inc.
Maxwell House, Fairview Park, Elmsford, N.Y. 10523

Pergamon of Canada Ltd.
207 Queen's Quay West, Toronto 117, Ontario

Pergamon Press Ltd.
Headington Hill Hall, Oxford

Pergamon Press (Aust.) Pty. Ltd.
Rushcutters Bay, Sydney, N.S.W.

Vieweg & Sohn GmbH
Burgplatz 1, Braunschweig

08 006867 7

CONTENTS

AUTHORS

MARVIN L. KAPLAN, Ph.D., Professor of Psychology, Department of Psychology, University of Windsor, Windsor, Ontario.

NICK J. COLARELLI, Ph.D., Associate Professor; Director, Institute for Organizational Psychology, St. Louis University, St. Louis, Mo.

RUTH BRILL GROSS, Ph.D., Assistant Professor, Departments of Psychiatry and Psychology; (Coordinator of Clinical Psychology Training, Cincinnati General Hospital), University of Cincinnati, Cincinnati, Ohio.

DONALD LEVENTHAL, Ph.D., Professor of Psychology and Director of Clinical Training, Bowling Green State University, Bowling Green, Ohio.

SAUL M. SIEGEL, Ph.D., Professor of Psychology and Director of Clinical Psychological Training; Professor, Department of Psychiatry, The Ohio State University, Columbus, Ohio.

PREFACE

The thought of producing a book on structural testing theory had its inception when the authors were colleagues at the Topeka State Hospital. While a beginning was made at that time, the impetus came later when we found ourselves teaching graduate clinical psychology students in university settings. At this point there was not the "environmental" support for the ego psychology approach to which we had been accustomed, and we more strongly felt the need of a text that set forth the system of theory and practice that we wished to teach. Our belief that such a text fills a gap in the literature on psychological testing needs explanation. It is our impression that many, if not all, of the concepts described here have been presented in the many available texts or compilations of readings in testing. However, it is also our impression that the many references to ego psychology or cognitive factors in personality fail to bring the relevant concepts into a cohesive or systematic framework that conveys their utility in understanding personality functioning, psychopathology, or their value in determining specific treatments for specific disturbances.

Our thinking and our subsequent formulations emerged out of the special atmosphere of the Topeka State Hospital and the influence of two great psychologists. The Hospital setting was one in which a spirit of pioneering and innovation was dominant, spirit that permitted staff of all disciplines to work together with a minimum of professional chauvinism. Information and ideas about patients and about treatment methods were listened to and efforts were made to carry out the treatment plans that were generated. A good description of the opportunity and challenge afforded in this setting is contained in Colarelli and Siegel's *Ward H: An Adventure in Innovation.*

In such a setting where opportunity brought demands and gave responsibility for the formulation of sound ideas and contributions from clinical psychologists, the clinicians were fortunate to have some guidance in working toward the goals of more effective service. Paramount in this was the more general influence of David Rapaport and the immediate hand of Austin M. DesLauriers. Rapaport had left Topeka in 1948 but his influence was still strongly felt. His image was that of a careful, thorough, theoretically sound clinician. Rapaport's efforts to systematize diagnostic testing within an ego psychology framework provided a foundation for our work. In his introduction to the recently revised edition of Rapaport, Gill, and Schafer's *Diagnostic Psychological Testing,* Holt conveys the qualities that Rapaport engendered in his students and colleagues. Among these was a respect for the clinician-psychologist as a theoretician upon whom it was incumbent to hold to logical consistency and to know the basis of his formulation.

DesLauriers, chief psychologist at the Topeka State Hospital from 1950 to 1958, was our immediate model of the clinician, the combination of intuitive psychologist and solid theoretician who knew enough depth psychology as well as academic psychology to be intelligently critical. He relished the challenge of demands for information and ideas and loved to expose depth psychology pronouncements which may have been poetic but which were valueless or misleading for the treatment of profoundly disturbed patients in a state hospital. In addition, DesLauriers thought through the contributions of the ego oriented psychoanalytic theoreticians and in *The Experience of Reality in Childhood Schizophrenia* placed them in a consistent framework with clear treatment implications. His views combined with some of our own elaborations of the writings of the ego psychologists form the structural approach that we present in this book.

In undertaking this book we have as our goal the presentation of an approach which we believe provides the closest and most fruitful linkage between testing and treatment. As will be mentioned repeatedly in the text, the emphasis on ego structure does not supplant a dynamic approach to test interpretation nor does it challenge the validity of such interpretation. Instead, our view is that information about personality dynamics must be evaluated in the context of a clear conceptualization of a given individual's structural makeup and the current status of ego factors. Where the personality is one with serious ego disturbance, ego structural concepts are preemptive — the immediate tasks of understanding and treatment require formulation of an adequate grasp of the ego disorganization, residual ego strength, and the impact of various kinds of treatment on that state of functioning. Where the patient's difficulties are not primarily derivations of ego disturbance, dynamic or conflict concepts will find greater utility.

This presentation of the structural approach is primarily concerned with the basic concepts involved rather than the implications for various types of personality or for the specific relationships of treatment possibilities to personality disturbances. While we have not delved into the vicissitudes of classification in psychodiagnosis, it is our belief that emphasis on dynamics has compounded the confusion and that the structural approach offers considerable hope of clearing the way for a more consistent and more meaningful diagnostic system. It is our hope that others, as well as ourselves, will further extend the approach being formulated into new areas of theory, research, and application.

Chapter I describes the structural approach and relates it historically to developments in psychology in general and clinical psychology specifically. The chapter addresses itself to the difficulty many readers will have in relating familiar concepts to a somewhat unfamiliar unifying framework and application to clinical practice.

In Chapter II we present a historical theoretical development which should orient psychoanalytically-minded psychologists as it traces the central thread of the evolution of thinking about the ego and the implications of variations in ego functioning for psychopathology. Less psychoanalytically-minded psychologists will hopefully recognize parallels in this emergence with changes in the thinking of academic psychology, for example, as traced by White in his series of articles on shifting conceptions of motivation (see White, 1959).

The chapter on testing, Chapter III, relates the structural approach to the practice of testing and gives a detailed appraisal of the implications of the approach for use in the clinical diagnostic examination. Again, clinicians will encounter the familiar in a framework that brings a number of testing concepts into a new perspective. This chapter begins to draw treatment concepts into relationship with structural ideas as they emerge from test inferences but stops short of a systematic analysis of such relationships.

In Chapter IV the authors apply structural concepts to schizophrenia in developing the theoretical framework of schizophrenia as faulty ego synthesis. The issues of ego impairment and ego adaptation are described as critical in determining where the schizophrenic patient is, what he needs, and where the "point of entry" for treatment occurs. Our selection of schizophrenia as the focal syndrome for this work is based on the reasoning that the differences in utility between structural and dynamic concepts are nowhere more critical than in the understanding and treatment of schizophrenia.

In Chapters V, VI, VII, and VIII the authors illustrate the structural approach by using case material. The intention here is not only to demonstrate that ego structural considerations are not limited to determining the presence or absence of schizophrenia or some other diagnostic category but also to give concrete data describing how structural concepts are elicited that are relevant to decisions regarding treatment. The four cases were selected for these chapters because they cover a fair range of qualities of functioning and thus more clearly bring into focus the common elements as well as contrasts between cases. As indicated earlier, it is our hope that similar structural analyses of other types of personality disturbance will be forthcoming and will contribute to a clearer and more meaningful classification system.

In addition to Austin DesLauriers, our gratitude goes to Heinz M. Graumann, current chief psychologist at the Topeka State Hospital, for his jolting reminders that we are humans trying to understand humans. We are also appreciative of the help of Alfred Paul Bay, Superintendent of Topeka State Hospital, who respected humans trying to understand humans. And to the humans whose struggle we hope to understand, we are always indebted.

The Authors

CHAPTER I

The Place and Importance of the Structural Approach in Psychological Evaluation

This book is based on the assumptions (a) that psychological evaluation provides a greater and more meaningful understanding of the patient, derived more quickly and more objectively than is possible through interviews and observation alone, and (b) that there are better and poorer choices of treatment contingent upon an understanding of the structural configuration and integrity of the patient's ego functioning. Determination of the relationship between these two assumptions, or principles of practice, can not only save time in treatment but also preclude certain dangers or hazards inherent in the application of inappropriate treatment.

To make the above statements at a time when individual psychodiagnostic testing appears to be on the decline (Holt, 1967) may seem to reflect an anachronistic blind faith. Indeed, Holt has presented an impressive argument to support his contention that "diagnostic testing today is in a funk" (p. 444). Few psychologists would argue with his observations that diagnostic testing is seen as a second-rate, low level skill in many settings, that many clinicians have lost faith in the value of testing even in relationship to therapy, that many psychologists feel uncomfortable with the "artistic" nature of psychodiagnosis and the use of instruments that appear to lack scientific validation, and that psychological evaluation has undergone a diminishing emphasis in professional meetings, publications, and graduate training programs. It has been the authors' experience that many clinical psychology graduate students see psychodiagnostic testing as one or both of two things: (a) a pre-therapy ritual in which a diagnostic label that has nothing to do with treatment is assigned, or presumed dynamic conflicts are revealed so as to protect the therapist from too many surprises and/or (b) an academic exercise which one must get through in order to go on to more interesting and important endeavors. Graduate students and professionals reflect to some extent the attitudes and teachings of their mentors and they, in turn, go on to influence the students for whom they become responsible. It would be easy to reach the conclusion that the prognosis for the future of diagnostic testing is indeed poor.

In agreement with Holt, we do not believe that the current status of testing is due to its demonstrated value or validity. We believe that there are developments which can change the current condition. A number of theoretical developments of recent years point the way for an even greater importance for psychodiagnostic evaluation and greater demands for psychologists who think in terms of new and more sophisticated dimensions (Holt, 1967; Kaplan, Hirt, and Kurtz, 1967). These developments have occurred in both psychoanalysis and academic psychology and have paralleled each other. Their emphasis has been upon the adaptive capacities of the human organism in relation to its environment. More specifically, theorists and researchers have turned their attention to " . . . the stable and pervasive characteristics in personality . . . usually called structural . . . which enable us to predict that people will respond differently to the same stimuli, press, or treatment" (Holt, 1967, p. 457).

If, as research rather convincingly demonstrates, these structural personality characteristics do determine differences in the effects of various treatments, then practice should reflect, insofar as is possible at this time, a recognition of this basic fact. The authors feel that there is a gap between what we consider good practice in psychodiagnostic work and the systems or approaches that are too often taught in graduate clinical psychology programs. Our goal is to describe an approach which we consider to reflect recent advances in ego psychology theory as it relates to new developments in therapeutic methodology. In doing this it is not our intention to supplant other approaches but to clarify the place of a method of using data which have greater value in understanding certain personalities and in relating test data to certain therapeutic contexts. By the structural approach, we refer to a view of personality as a system of adaptive functioning which has these properties: (a) mental processes that are organized in relationship to the organism's reality adaptive experiences and (b) the hierarchical organization of such processes.

In viewing personality as an organizational system we are lending emphasis to what has been subsumed under "cognition," styles of perceptual defense, coping or defensive systems, ego strength (or resiliency), and reality contact. All of these terms refer to the structural aspects of personality, in contrast to its contents which can be viewed as personality dynamics. Under the latter term are included specific conflicts (e.g., activity vs. passivity, strivings toward heterosexuality vs. fear of castration, etc.) and the derivatives of such conflicts as they emerge in all aspects of behavior including, of course, interpersonal relationships. These latter factors are not unimportant; rather, our concern is that in the thrill of discovering depth motivation explanations for behavior, we have taken care of only a small proportion of the factors that explain behavior. The themes that have emerged to deal with "depth" or dynamic psychology may not be wrong but they appear to us to overshoot the critical problems that psychologists frequently encounter: of what kinds of functioning is a person capable? under what conditions will this functioning emerge? what stratagems can be employed to alter these contingencies?

FORCES AND DEVELOPMENTS IN PSYCHOLOGICAL TESTING

The major methodological issues with which clinical psychology has wrestled during the past twenty years appear to be abating in intensity. However, this does not mean that these issues have been resolved or that solutions are in prospect. Indeed, it appears that clinical psychology is reaching some level of harmony with itself, with the rest of psychology, and with other professions, by finding new common ground relatively free from conflict. These developments are positive in the sense of showing promise of encouraging the professional to draw more freely from theory and research within a broad range of behavior science. Psychological testing, however, appears to have been trapped in the unresolved conflicts, and its development and reintegration into modern clinical work is hampered.

Some recent articles have attempted to place these professional events in perspective (Anastasi, 1967; Holt, 1967; Kaplan, Hirt, and Kurtz, 1967). From the frame of reference with which we are concerned at the moment — forces that determine theoretical orientations to psychological testing — it is important to describe some of these developments.

The early entrenchment of "methods" of scoring and interpreting tests

While some of the early test developers were psychiatrists, it was clearly the psychologists who took to test methodology. Tests offered the possibility of forming an amalgam of experimental method and clinical application. Standardized test items plus standardized administrative procedures could be perceived as independent variables, while the patient's responses were scorable results along dimensions of dependent variables. Moreover, by accumulating and comparing test data of subjects who were drawn from certain populations identifiable by other criteria (e.g., psychiatric classification, psychosomatic illness), it was possible to utilize tests as a research tool. However, one of the requirements in these procedures was to reduce test results to quantifiable data so that the demand for scientific measurement could be met. The traditions of psychology were not easily satisfied by arguments for an intuitive approach. Respected professionals, as well as graduate students, cringed at being identified with people who were able to look over test results and expound on the psychopathology revealed, but who could not tie their inferences to testable deductions.

Not only were clearly defined scoring systems closer to scientific requirements but this aspect of testing was easier to teach. Novice clinical students could be taught an approach to projective testing that provided a context of procedure and methods of inference which offered a "safe" framework of operation while the student learned to deal with patients in clinical settings. What emerged was Rorschach "theory" or Thematic Apperception Test "theory" or the various interpretive schemes that developed for each of the tests. Rapaport's comment (1952) was disturbing but incisive: test results were interpreted piecemeal and "dished up in more or less of a hash" (p. 462). Mature clinicians tended to form their own scoring systems and their own more or less integrated frameworks of personality theory that seemed operative. In many cases, this was "eclectic" but psychoanalytically oriented and in the hands of a good many clinicians the approach which evolved probably had consistency, depth, and thoroughness. It is noteworthy, however, that these clinicians were unable to develop any means of mutual support or communication beyond their immediate contacts with students or colleagues in workshops. No journals emerged that encouraged the expansion of clinical testing theory. Correspondingly, clinical psychology itself was not developing along the lines of classifying or reformulating theories of personality, psychopathology, or a broad systematic test theory. Almost all of the clinical psychologists who have made contributions to theories of psychopathology did so completely out of the context of the stream of clinical thinking (e.g., Mowrer) and usually in the stream of psychoanalytic thinking (e.g., Holt; Rapaport; Schafer).

This problem of entrenchment of technology and insulation from endeavors to develop valid and explicable theories of psychopathology has perpetuated an anachronistic system in testing. Perhaps the clearest statement of theoretical advances in the two decades from 1940 to 1960 was White's (1959) elucidation of the evolution of the concept of adaptive behavior in both academic psychology and psychoanalysis. In the decade since White's paper, the term "ego psychology" has become popular, but efforts to revise test concepts in terms of this new "mainstream" are almost totally lacking.

Role models and psychologist identity

Graduate students in clinical psychology must joke about the irrelevance of research results to clinical practice in order to deal with their discomfort regarding the contradictions. But the discomfort is deep and not easily dispelled. In their internships the students are under the tutelage of clinicians operating professionally and frequently at a geographic as well as administrative distance from the university. This experience confronts the trainee with conflicting goals. If the trainee aspires to become an applied clinical psychologist, the clinician in the field is the immediate model for identification. The clinician's methods, working assumptions, and approach to clinical tasks require the student to compartmentalize academic and clinical viewpoints. The clinical psychology faculty based in the university often offers no middle ground; these psychologists are frequently relieved that the clinical training is removed from the academic setting, thus presenting less of a threat to them in this struggle to maintain a scientific posture to gain status and acceptance among their academic colleagues.

The research that has been done on the validity of diagnostic instruments has almost exclusively been carried out by such academic clinical psychologists or, under their direction, by students working on dissertation projects. The research has focused, understandably, on checking the validity of the systems that crystallized as early efforts to make the whole business scientific. As Holt (1967) has indicated, the statements by the early experts as to what certain variables meant was taken as if each relationship must have a validity of its own, demonstrable in isolation from a complex judgmental process. When these initial efforts failed to support the clinician's stand, the clinicians fell back on the principle that test inferences were based on the configurational principle; that is, configurations of scores were presumed to be the keys to interpretation. Holt points out that even efforts to test this approach did not work out because so little work has been done on determining just how expert clinicians actually work. To quote Holt (1967, p. 453),

> A few masters of testing (for example, Schafer, 1949) have had the insight to see that the only validational research that made much sense used clinical judgments, not objective test scores, as predictors. Most of the positive results have been obtained in studies of this kind . . .

The promise of ego psychology

Psychological testing lost the aura of mystique with which it was earlier enveloped, and many psychologists and students were disillusioned and cynical. Concomitantly, there were other developments in psychology that stirred interest and enthusiasm. Among the recent developments has been the interest in cognitive styles. This interest emerged through the development of research methodology that appeared to embrace and absorb the concepts of psychological testing, especially those of projective testing. Shortly after World War II, a movement called the "New Look in Perception" sought through research to determine the relationships between dynamic aspects of personality and more immediate or observable behavioral concomitants. These included such investigations as the relationship between need (or deprivation) and perception of size of valued objects or the relationship between styles of defense (as observed in the Rorschach) and varieties of perceptual style (as "leveling" and "sharpening"; see Klein, 1951).

This area of interest appears to have merged with a second trend, namely, the resurgence of interest in early environmental influence. As Hunt (1961) has pointed out, the key concept has shifted from the question of environmental versus hereditary influence to questions regarding the nature of the interaction. This interest has focused on the nature of the organism's relationship to his environment as a factor in the emergence of cognitive abilities as well as specific "personality" attributes.

In all of this work one dominant theme has become clear. In both psychoanalytic thinking and in psychological research the formulations have moved toward conceptions of the nature of the organism's adaptive structuring. In psychoanalytic theorizing there has been a remarkable shift from emphasis on "id" forces, early traumatic events, and genetically based conflicts, toward greater understanding of the development of the ego and its resources for coping with stress. As White (1959) has nicely demonstrated, the change parallels that in academic psychology where the early focus on stimulus-response connections and a tension reduction model of reinforcement has been gradually replaced by motivational concepts of "effectance," competence, or mastery.

Interest in both psychoanalysis and psychology has moved toward more sophisticated models of understanding individual differences in terms of early experience. It now appears not only possible, but acceptable, to theorize about personality in terms other than those of fixations at psychosexual stages or genetic conflicts.

Structural and dynamic conceptions as complementary

The psychoanalytic framework has up to recently been used almost exclusively in terms of its dynamic connotations. That is, it has been used as if it were a system describing intrapsychic forces. Defenses have been conceived as reactive patterns to control certain internal pressures or strivings that emanated from fears of the events that would ensue if control was lost. In this system, symptom formation was viewed as something like skin eruptions — surface manifestations incidental to the disturbance but perhaps secondarily leading to distress in the environment. This archaic model of psychoanalysis yielded to a modified version which recognized certain behavior as defensive but the defense was still a relic of the person's infantile history — the defensive mode was one fixed in early childhood as the effort to avoid anxiety associated with internal conflict. A model with more current acceptance considers not only the "individual's" view of himself, his perception of the environment, and his efforts at defense or coping as having been molded by early experiences, but also views these factors — self-view, perception of the external world, and defense and coping resources — as in a continual interaction with changes in an emerging equilibrium or evolving character development as the person matures.

As much as this model appears to be a more flexible and useful tool in understanding personality, there are still some supplemental considerations needed which we refer to as "structural concepts." Rapaport (1951) makes the distinction between energy-dynamic concepts and those of structure; the former refer to drives, drive conflicts, and drive vicissitudes; the latter refer to thresholds of discharge, control systems, and integrative patternings. Structural concepts may be viewed analogously to the framework of a building — the basic design, materials, and mode of construction; dynamic concepts can be compared to the character of the building's use — room layout, special uses of the space, and traffic patterns. Some buildings have problems because of "structural" deficiencies and attention to room layout is no remedy; some buildings need "therapy" for relatively contextual problems such as the more appropriate or harmonious use of space.

Structural concepts in relationship to functions of testing

In terms of personality assessment, the appropriate level of concern depends on the nature of a person's dysfunction and the goals of testing. In Chapter III we describe four levels of testing oriented around the nature of the questions being asked and the kinds of personality variables that need to be considered in answering such questions.

An area in which the problem of proper focus or balance between structural and dynamic concepts is of great concern is the treatment of "borderline" patients. One of the great concerns of therapists who treat patients on an out-patient basis is the uneasiness they have regarding the subtle or hidden aspects of the patient's ego integrity. In the structural framework an effort is made to grasp the nature of a patient's ego problems even when he is apparently functioning at a relatively adequate level. The key point here is that patients with ego defects are not merely people with poor functioning but that many of these individuals have been able to make more or less successful adaptations to their defects. The structural emphasis brings into perspective the fluctuation of mental organization in patients with ego defects and relates the fluctuation to degree of impairment, degree of strain imposed by the environment, and capacity for adaptive compensation (Kaplan, 1967). In situations where a patient does not show overt signs of disorganization, it is possible to determine the degree to which the patient is attempting to deal with, or control, or compensate for ego defect. In the cases analyzed in the latter part of this book, there are considerations such as the restricted span or unit of experience or behavior, the seeking and utilizing of external causes or input, the heightened focus on experiences of intensity, and the development of meta-concepts that transcend "reality" and help a patient organize his experience into "parallel" or pseudo-reality form. A number of these patternings remind us of the organic's effort to protect himself from experiences that would strain his resources (see Kaplan, 1964). In principle, the person with poor ego integration seeks the same goals as "normals" although the efforts he makes and the adaptations that emerge have distinctive quality in terms of the specific threats or dangers he feels and his use of his specific resources.

The following is an illustration of the problem of determining the proper place of dynamic and structural concepts, a problem frequently encountered in psychotherapy:

Mr. S. has been seen in individual psychotherapy at an out-patient clinic for three years. His clinical symptomatology includes anxiety and a combination of voyeurism and exhibitionism. This man's clinical history is rich in dynamics, involving a very complex parental relationship, rivalry with an older brother who was physically, although not intellectually, superior to him, and the occurrence of several traumatic events in earlier life. Much of the psychotherapy has focused upon a search, via the transference relationship, for a meaning of these symptoms. The psychotherapy appears to have been conducted intelligently and with consistency, yet there has been little in the way of positive results. During the course of a recent re-evaluation using psychological testing it became obvious that the symptoms were not, as had been assumed, an attempt to symbolically reinforce the presence of a penis or more general masculinity in this man, but rather an attempt on the part of the patient to reassure himself and to counter the panic associated with dangers of depersonalization and a reaction to a schizophrenic sense of "not existing." From a content analysis point of view the test material lent itself well to a dynamic interpretation and this had been the basis for the psychotherapy. The re-evaluation re-opened the question of the basic intactness of the ego organization and lent a new interpretation to the symptoms and the underlying panic involved. The specific recommendations for therapy were now stated in terms of greater emotional giving on the part of the therapist and more general ego support via this relationship.

This example indicates the limitations that may be involved in a purely dynamic interpretation of the test material. Such an interpretation frequently does not come to grips with the quality of ego functioning and presupposes the effectiveness of treatment focused on dynamics. Where ego impairment is evident, the emphasis on dynamics must be abated and concern must be shifted to the establishing and supporting of ego integration. The interpretation of test material, by revealing the nature of pathology in a broader context, helped direct treatment toward proper goals.

RELEVANCE OF THE STRUCTURAL
APPROACH IN TREATMENT

In psychoanalytically oriented psychotherapy, the essence of treatment is the analysis of the transference relationship. By giving minimum clarity or "visibility" to his own personality, the therapist may assume that the patient's perception of him is a function of the patient's personality rather than his own. This approach presupposes a unified integrated ego on the part of the patient, and problems arise if this presumption is not correct. When integration is lacking, and there is a breakdown or structural impairment in the functioning of the patient's perceptual and cognitive apparatus, the distortion with which the patient views the therapist is no longer solely based upon unconscious motives. Instead, it is based upon a combination of such motives and the additional distortions introduced by faulty ego organization. In the treatment of the patient lacking such an integration, the transference relationship becomes an inadequate frame of reference when used by itself (Knight, 1954). With lack of ego integration there is invariably some degree of breakdown in reality functions. The patient has difficulty in reality testing. When his environment permits, he counters the panic accompanying this phenomenon by attempting to take restitutional steps that serve to re-establish cohesiveness. These steps may be physical or verbal but, in any event, they are aimed at fostering feedback or controlling the environment; the behavior is geared toward compensating for ego impairment. In psychotherapy, to provide a "blank screen" for such a patient is to deprive him of the use of such adaptive resources. If this does not invite the disaster of a pathological disorganization, it at least prevents progress.

The alternative to providing an ambiguous transference-stimulating figure for the patient is to provide optimum reality feedback. This requires that the therapist present an unambiguous behavioral picture of himself. Clear, open behavior by the therapist serves to give clear indications of reality to the patient and gives the patient a "real" person with whom to interact. Through this experience, the patient's weakened ego processes may be supported. This is not to say that interpretations are never of value in such situations. They may be supportive of the patient's logical intellectual processes provided that interpretations are at a level that can be comprehended and integrated by the patient's ego. The goal of interpretation, as of other therapeutic maneuvers, is to help the patient master or coordinate inner functioning and its relationship to outer reality. The psychotherapeutic treatment of the patient with ego defects is not a "hand-holding" operation nor just an exercise in trying to maintain a patient at his present level of functioning and so preclude regression into more severe disturbance. It is no less difficult than traditional psychoanalytic therapy and, in fact, may demand as much if not more personal commitment, patience, creative innovation, and adherence to basic theoretical principles, as does therapy with well-integrated neurotics.

A number of recent publications have developed the theme of ego-psychological relevant factors in treatment. DesLauriers (1962), while chief psychologist at Topeka State Hospital during the early 1950's, developed a theory of treatment based on his work with chronic and childhood schizophrenics. For DesLauriers, schizophrenia is indicative of a step missed in the maturation of a child, the step in which he learns the boundaries of his body and then of his ego (i.e., the hierarchy of integrated organizations of experience that provide the personality with the capacity to act, synthesize experience, and adapt to reality in a meaningful and gratifying manner). In other words, schizophrenia is a matter of incomplete personality structure, not a retreat from reality. The word "reality" occurs time and again in the context of ego psychological theory and may be disturbing for those who consider the philosophical difficulties inherent in defining this term insurmountable. DesLauriers, however, assumes that in the process of normal development, an individual learns what is self and not self and learns to feel himself to be a relatively consistent entity limited in space and continuous in time. The individual who cannot achieve or maintain such identity has difficulty encountering reality. DesLauriers also assumes that the only true gratifications are to be found in self acting upon the world outside oneself and that individuals strive for real, rather than fantasy, gratifications and a resultant sense of personal reality. Therefore, the process of "recovery" for the schizophrenic is contingent upon reinstating those conditions necessary for experiencing reality and relationships. The therapist can make no assumptions about the capacity of the "very ill" chronic schizophrenic or the schizophrenic child to enter into a relationship; instead he begins with the belief that the patient is unable to engage in a relationship as ordinarily conceived. The therapist must become an intrusive presence, a concrete model for the individual, a helper but also one who requires the patient to learn to respond and to grow and assume increasing responsibility (Colarelli and Siegel, 1966). As illustrated by Colarelli and Siegel (1966), DesLauriers (1962), and Freeman, Cameron, and McGhie (1958), the treatment operations will change as the patient progresses to higher levels of functioning, but the basic principle – mastery of reality and strengthening of adaptive functions – remains the same.

Hollon (1966) and Knight (1953) have also provided ego psychological concepts relevant to the treatment of "borderline" and depressed patients. Although these authors concern themselves primarily with out-patient therapy in the articles mentioned, the principles are adaptable to in-patient treatment, as discussed elsewhere by Hollon (1965). Principles shared by the two authors include the importance of the therapist providing "borrowed" or "lend lease" ego strength for his patient when the patient is not capable of providing his own intention, initiative, direction, and controls. Because these patients lack certain (executive and synthetic) ego capacities which enable hardier individuals to function autonomously in the face of stress, frustration, and interpersonal difficulties, the therapist takes an active role in directing the patient's focus to factors which lead to disruption. This involves the learning of new, adaptive, and practical ways of dealing with these disruptions and maintaining organization and control. These are also important considerations for patients who have left a hospital setting but still need supportive therapeutic care.

While statements can be made about individual psychotherapy, equally important statements can be made about broader areas of treatment. In hospital settings the physical, social, and cultural influences that the institution brings to bear upon the patient are basically oriented to the structural aspects of the personality. The person who becomes acutely ill and hospitalized in a psychiatric facility has frequently lost the ability to meaningfully relate that which goes on about him to the feelings and thoughts he possesses. In the case of severe depression, this collapse may be seen in the context of the patient's incapacity to deal with overwhelming aggressive impulses and strong regressive oral drives, as well as in a loss of ego organization. In schizophrenia this is seen as a withdrawal or loss of cathexis from ego functions and resultant disorganization. A patient may have delusions that he is part of a communist conspiracy; he may fear a homosexual attack, or have frankly incestuous desires. Any one of these thoughts and fears may be subject to dynamic analysis and fit into a carefully developed genetic formulation. However, for the immediate treatment process in both kinds of pathology, there is a loss of ego organization and the need for protection and procedures which lead to reintegration. Milieu treatment can provide a temporary crutch for the ego, offering initially an environment of order or "structure" that reduces stimuli to a less complex level, thus reducing strain on ego processes. Later there can be a phasing or gradual shift encouraging the functioning of basic adaptive ego systems in relation to the environment.

It is specifically in the area of discovering where, how, and under what circumstances the ego will be able to assume some mastery, that testing adds an invaluable contribution. In hospitals, the physical, social, and interpersonal contexts are rich in therapeutic potential. As the range of therapeutic possibilities is discriminated more finely and translated with some innovation, initiative, and imagination, treatment agencies discover that they have untapped resources which are directly related to adaptive or ego functions. The use of ego-relevant theory and principles in the treatment of institutionalized patients is exemplified in Colarelli and Siegel's (1966) *Ward H,* Cumming and Cumming's (1966) *Ego and Milieu,* and Freeman, Cameron, and McGhie's (1958) *Chronic Schizophrenia.* Although the theoretical approaches are couched in somewhat different terms in each volume, these books share an emphasis on the therapeutic potency of the milieu (including staff, especially aides and nurses), the belief that ego growth and organization can be fostered through planned, graduated problem-solving on the part of the patients, and the necessity for maintaining a consistent, stable staff who are capable of giving of themselves and providing role models. These presentations make quite clear the importance of translating theoretical principles into very concrete operations such as making sure that patients can see calendars and clocks (to reinstitute a sense of time), have enough soap (to renew their personal care), and have clothes which are individually possessed and not group property (patients need individual possessions to help re-establish an identity), to name a few perhaps less exciting but extremely important examples. Likewise, group activities and discussion are of value for patients who have lost or have never learned the capacity to relate to others and to understand the roles and feelings of other people. Physical activity is equally important in helping many patients gain a sense of bodily functioning (i.e., physical ego boundaries) as well as helping to reinstate some basic, concrete patterns of behavior.

The value of productive activity is generally recognized but perhaps needs re-emphasis and interpretation as a therapeutic vehicle. Work assignments have two main advantages. They place patients within organizations or systems that generally have clear goal-oriented structures and methods and they provide the opportunity for identity-enhancing experiences. A number of enlightened hospitals bring their industrial, maintenance, and service departments into the therapeutic fold so that the entire institution is truly an organic unity devoted to patient interest. This system has the capacity for graded placements of patients where the kinds of tasks, the degree of structure, the demands of the job, and the nature of supervisory relationship can be taken into consideration in meeting the patient's needs for organization, stimulation, challenge, appropriate identity models, or even the patient's need to perceive himself as a useful human being. In the graded task system, the hospital can adapt the patient's placements to conform to his growing capacity to function more independently.

Using test data for therapeutic planning

The structural approach extrapolates from psychological test data to concepts relevant to therapeutic intervention. Intactness of ego functions, specific assets and liabilities, and modes of interaction with reality are concepts which can be spelled out and used in making specific recommendations. The number of questions that can be formulated from the test material and specifically related to treatment are legion. The following are examples of a few of these questions together with the kind of treatment directions that may be indicated. To what extent is there internal organization within the person? Is the patient able to organize the stimuli that impinge upon him? The extent to which the individual is in fact incapable of organizing these sensations indicates the degree to which the therapist, the milieu, or other aspects of the treatment process must take the responsibility for doing this for him in order to reach a point where his own functioning can be reinstituted. A similar question may be posed regarding how well the patient is capable of controlling his impulses toward the environment. Here, too, the treatment program must consider the range of possibilities for outbursts and ways in which outbursts may be controlled and responded to in the most constructive way, i.e., how the environment can best provide feedback about the effect of the patient's behavior and impose control rather than purposeless punitive reaction. A related question refers to the sense of "emptiness" that the patient might feel. "Emptiness" is the patient's sense of lack of meaning, a by-product of disorganiza-tion. In this area it would again be the responsibility of the therapist or of some other person in the treatment program to make decisions regarding appropriate ways to make an impact upon the patient and to help him relate the resulting feelings with the realities of life.

A broader aspect of these same questions is how the individual experiences himself and the world. It will be part of our task to bring a certain range of phenomenological experience into the explanatory framework of the structural approach. Our basic conception is that experience is mediated by the current condition of personality structure and that variations in structure produce variations in experience. Experience itself, in a phenomenological sense, is not only a product of organization but can have a strong stimulating and motivating property that, in turn, can affect a person's behavior and functioning. From this point of view, it becomes quite important to direct attention toward encouraging or discouraging situations and events that foster certain experiences. For example, it may prove quite crucial that we permit a young man to select a project and to complete it without help so that he may gain the experience of self-direction and mastery and thus regain portions of experience associated with his functioning as a male with an acceptable role definition. It should be noted that in the theoretical scheme, structure, functioning, and experience are only conceptual foci for examining the same phenomena.

There are still other test-relevant questions which must be considered. Does the patient respond to the affect qualities of his interaction with the environment as against the content part of it? The answer to this dictates a specific approach to him in the therapeutic process. Also what is the patient's capacity to deal with nuances in the environment about him? If psychological testing indicates that the patient is capable of responding only to the grosser aspects of his relationships with others and the total environment, a specific direction would be suggested in at least an initial approach to him. This question, in turn, may be related to a broader one: what do the tests tell us about how the patient responds to language? The psychoses are generally accompanied by a loss in abstract attitude, either partially or completely, and in such a situation, even apparently intact language functioning has a different meaning for the patient than for someone who is more integrated. Suggestions regarding the relevance of language for the patient may indicate to what extent and at what level (concrete or more abstract) the patient is capable of integrating linguistic communication. In instances in which we discover that patients can understand only concrete responses, concentration on a totally verbal therapeutic approach will lack effectiveness. In this same area, specific suggestions could be made about the extent to which physical contact is appropriate in approaching and making an impact upon the patient as against the more verbal aspects of the treatment process. To emphasize this point, it is certainly conceivable for the psychologist to make specific suggestions regarding the appropriateness of individual or group psychotherapy, milieu treatment, degree of structure necessary for life experience within an institution or outside of an institution, or the various combinations of these that might be appropriate in a particular situation. All of these questions relate to the problem of translating test behavior to inferences regarding the relationship between the patient's ego functioning and relevant environmental conditions that may be employed discriminatingly for therapeutic advantage.

In general, these questions relate to the patient's needs at the time he is being approached for treatment and the treatment plan that can best fit these needs. Any treatment plan would, of course, be at best tentative and require trial, observation, and correction but, at the same time, it would provide general direction to areas that need to be approached in the treatment and as a basis for prediction.

In summary, our thesis is that ego-impaired individuals initially require treatment oriented to the development of ego autonomy and only after some level of autonomous functioning has been achieved can attention be turned toward dynamic or conflict problems. The diagnostic process, to be useful, must be related to this need and this cannot be the case when the personality description is limited to the problems of intrapsychic conflict.

In closing this chapter, we should like to quote from Kenneth Keniston:

> For psychoanalysts . . . the ego is the organizing, governing, co-ordinating center of personality, whose primary tasks are to maintain psychic harmony and to 'adapt' to the demands and possibilities of the environment. In performing these tasks, the ego has at its disposal a variety of functions: defense, synthesis, dissociation, assimilation, timing, perception, intentions, reality-testing, anticipation, differentiation, automatization, and a host of others. Ego 'breakdown' occurs when the ego 'regresses' to more primitive and less differentiated levels of functioning, relies on more childlike and less adaptive defense, and becomes incapable of the fine accommodations and subtle compromises which can characterize ego functioning at its best.

> Whatever our ultimate judgment about the scientific validity of psychoanalytic ego psychology, the development of this new field reflects the major demands of technological society ... (in which) ... the most visible pathologies arise in those who cannot attain the requisite levels of ego functioning .... It is no accident that psychoanalytic ego psychology has been most highly developed in the most technological nation in the world. (1965, pp. 364-5)

Concomitant with demanding a high level of ego functioning as Keniston suggests, our society no longer provides the kinds of support which formerly enabled many ego-deficient individuals to find acceptable roles. Beyond the more circumscribed area of treatment intervention for those who come for therapy or hospitalization, the broader concern of the ego-oriented social scientist is the development of social systems and institutions whereby the potentialities of children and adults can be supported and developed to the fullest. Thus, the ego psychological approach is congruent with a broad philosophy of community mental health on one hand, and the rehabilitation of the physically and psychologically handicapped, on the other.

CHAPTER II

Psychoanalytic Foundations of the Structural Theory

In this Chapter, an effort will be made to enunciate and clarify those aspects of psychoanalytic ego theory requisite to the structural approach. First, the concept of ego will be traced historically in the psychoanalytic literature with attention being focused upon the elaborations and refinements that this concept has undergone since Freud. Secondly, the relevant stages of ego development and integration will be described. Our goal is to present a clear ego psychology framework within which our test material can be comprehended.

THEORETICAL DEVELOPMENT OF THE CONCEPT OF EGO

Between 1919 and 1923, Freud recast his theoretical perspective into a new conceptual scheme. In *The Ego and The Id* (1923) he divided personality into three hypothetical mental structures — the ego, the id, and the superego. The id was equated with what Freud had previously termed "the system unconscious," that is, the reservoir of instinctual life. The superego was equated with conscience, with recognition of the fact that much of the superego was also unconscious. The ego was defined as that part of the personality which was in close contact with the outside world. It differed from the id in that primarily it was an organization, whereas the id was characterized by lack of organization.

The ego as executor

In describing the ego as the organized part of the id, Freud stated, "We have here formulated the idea that in every individual there is a coherent organization of mental processes, which we shall call his ego" (1923, p. 211). For Freud, the ego had both conscious and unconscious elements, and hence, while the awareness of "self" was a property of the ego, it could not be equated with it. The matrix of the ego was to be found in the multitude of internal and external perceptions which arise from the body and particularly from its surface. It included the part processes of perception, memory, control of motility, reality testing, and secondary process thinking. In this conception, Freud primarily considered the ego as the executive agency of the personality. It was the ego which set up the goals of the personality, delineated the means by which these goals were to be achieved, and harnessed the necessary energy for achievement.

The ego and synthesis

Nunberg (1930) elaborated upon another ego function which he termed the "synthetic" function. This capacity of the ego manifests itself through assimilating disparate mental elements, both from within and without the person. The synthetic function operates through mediating opposing elements, reconciling opposites, and setting mental productivity in motion. Nunberg suggested that this capacity grew out of the ego's tendency to unify and connect because of its intolerance of excessive contradictions. By virtue of this function, the most heterogeneous psychic elements are combined and often fused with impressions from the outside world to form new structures. It is this function that impels man to the harmonious unification of his strivings in which the ego acts as an intermediary and binding force. This tendency to unite, combine, and create goes hand in hand with the tendency to simplify and to generalize.

Nunberg pointed out that it is the synthetic function which brings about an integrated, harmonious relationship between the id, the superego, and external reality — a relationship that permits the individual to meet his needs and to seek gratification and growth within the limits of the physical and social environment. As the ego is the "master gland" of the psychic apparatus, it is possible to conceive of the synthetic function as the "master gland" of the ego. It integrates the basic psychological processes of the human being not only in terms of the immediate moment but also over time. It condenses and fixes the locus of experience within the confines of the organism's physical being. The synthetic function evaluates incoming sensory data, compares it to previous experiences, and organizes behavior, thereby enabling the ego to adapt and to cumulatively absorb experiences throughout an individual's life. This active, evaluating, and absorbing function enables the ego to define and determine the manner in which it will respond to future experiences and also to reinterpret past experiences. It is in this way that the ego, searching, probing, and considering the chaos of sensory input, is able to organize itself, utilize current experiences to reorganize and interpret past experiences, and create its own goals. The synthetic function enables the ego to "lay its own tracks" for the future and "re-lay the tracks" of the past. The synthetic function, therefore, serves as an anchor, a basic frame of reference from which the personality experiences its current condition, re-evaluates old experiences, sets up goals, and implements a plan of action for future adaptations.

The synthetic process is the nuclear function of the ego. It is through this function that the ego approaches internal and external experiences in a gestalt-like fashion, unique to the individual and the individual's history, and molds for the personality its characteristic, unique mode of functioning that we generally term "character style." As Rapaport pointed out, the integration which provides thought organization, the imprint of individuality, is one aspect of the synthetic function of the ego (1951, p. 662).

In relation to the external world, the synthetic function enables the ego to establish, in Federn's terms, a "sense of reality" (1952). This inner experiential map is a reflection of the individual's integration of the impact of the world, interpreted, and possibly distorted, in terms of his unique approach. This aspect of the synthetic function serves an economic purpose in that it enables the personality to react discriminatingly to the stimuli impinging upon the sensorium. It frees the personality from the burden of constant reality testing of each incoming stimulus. It permits the organism to respond to the familiar without conscious effort, thus making more energy available for reality testing in other areas.

The ego and adaptation

A new phase in the study of the ego was initiated by Hartmann and described in *Ego Psychology and the Problem of Adaptation* (1939). He pointed out that the clinical material elicited in therapeutic psychoanalysis underscored the importance of the instinctual drives and the environment as the two main factors in ego development. Conflict between the drives and reality resulted in the appearance of new features with the ego. However, Hartmann found it difficult to conceive that every ego function was the result of conflict, especially since the ego serves the purpose of adaptation to the environment.

He theorized that there must be a conflict-free development of many ego functions or part processes such as perception, intention, perceptual constancy, recall, motor development, language, thought, and perhaps others. He was careful to point out that this did not mean that these ego functions whose origin was conflict-free might not secondarily be drawn into a relationship with conflictual elements. The term "conflict-free ego sphere" was suggested for these functions insofar as they exerted their initial effect outside the realm of psychic conflict. Implicit in this construction is the theory that the ego has independent origins. These origins are not identical in substance with the id although Hartmann theorized that both id and ego arise from a common, undifferentiated matrix of inborn endowment. As Hartmann stated:

> In introducing his concepts of psychic structure, Freud speaks of a gradual differentiation of the ego from the id .... Freud's formulation has obvious disadvantages. It implies that the infant's equipment existing at birth is part of the id. It seems, however, that the innate apparatus and reflexes cannot all be part of the id, in the sense generally accepted in psychoanalysis. We suggest a different assumption, namely that of an undifferentiated phase during which both the id and the ego gradually are formed ... The new formulation permits a better explanation of some of the basic properties of both id and ego. During the undifferentiated phase there is maturation of apparatuses that later will come under the control of the ego, and that serve motility, perception, and certain thought processes. Maturation in these areas proceeds without the total organization we call ego; only after ego-formation will these functions be fully integrated. To the degree to which differentiation takes place man is equipped with a specialized organ of adaptation, that is, with the ego (1951, pp. 376–7).

During development, the ego falls heir to the inborn equipment that comprises the perceptual apparatus, the muscular system, intentionality, object comprehension, thinking, language, recall phenomena and learning. This is not to state that these functions are given as fully matured. Initially, they are presented only nascently and Hartmann implies that they develop:

(a)   as functional changes of more primitive apparatuses,

(b)   as new apparatuses arising in the course of development, and

(c)   as the maturation of apparatuses which together with the drive constitution are ontogenetic givens.

Hartmann refers to these functions which originate in the "hereditary core" of the ego as primary autonomous factors in ego development. By this, he means that these factors enter into the final outcome of the ego as independent variables. His hypothesis suggests that any consideration of ego development must take four factors into account: first, the impact of reality; second, the instinctual drives; third, the influence of the autonomous factors originating in the hereditary material and their maturational laws; and finally, the equilibrium established by the synthetic function, which must integrate these prior three factors and the remainder of the ego.

In contrast with the primary autonomous functions, Hartmann indicated that there are many other ego characteristics such as personality traits, behavior patterns, mannerisms, etc., which may have a relative independence from conflict and regressive tendencies. He stated that behavior which arose originally in the service of defense against a drive may, in the course of time, become an independently working structure. The original energy invested in these trait structures was derived from the id, but as these traits become automatized and lose their defensive function, the energy is neutralized and is taken over by the ego for adaptive purposes. Hartmann states, "It cannot be a matter of 'chance' that automatisms play so great a role among these processes which are either directly adaptive or are used by adaptation processes. It is obvious that automatization may have economic advantages, by saving attention-cathexes in particular and conscious-cathexes in general. In using automatisms we apply already existing means, the structure of which we need not create anew at every occasion, and consequently some of the means-end relations can be, so to speak, taken for granted . . . . " (1951, p. 393). Here Hartmann means that neither internal nor external stresses result in a deterioration of certain ego traits. Hartmann names this tendency towards relative stability, "secondary autonomy."

These secondary autonomous factors are most vulnerable to stress in childhood. As Anna Freud (1952) has pointed out, the stability of the secondary autonomous elements, especially in childhood, is dependent upon the child's object relations. It is the bond of the love object that enforces the neutralization of id energy and prevents the disintegration of the ego behavior into its original instinctual form. Hartmann has indicated that the degree of secondary autonomy must vary from individual to individual and must be of great importance in determining relative ego strength. It is out of the gradual accumulation of capacities, adaptive functions, and sub-organizations (termed secondary autonomous functions) that the synthetic ego begins to lay down the basic framework which is later to be identified as character, personality, and the enduring style or habit of approach to oneself and the world.

It is useful at this point to clarify that the development of primary and secondary autonomous functions does not occur in clear-cut, mutually exclusive stages. Rather, while the beginning of the development of primary autonomous functions must necessarily precede the secondary, the development is not entirely distinct but tends to overlap and be interactive. It might then be said that the development of primary autonomous functions defines and determines the development of secondary autonomous functioning, but at the same time the development of secondary autonomous functions in one area may facilitate or inhibit the development of primary autonomous functions in other areas. One might speculate that in an infant who has learned to respond to anxiety through motor expression, precocious development in this direction might actually impede the development of other forms of response to anxiety. Conversely, a proclivity for rumination and thinking may particularly further the development of the capacity for delay.

The ego as locus of experience

Paul Federn (1952) further elucidated and developed the role of the ego in the basic picture of psychic functioning laid down by Freud. Federn has enabled us to conceive of the ego, not as merely a conceptual abstraction, but as a process which mediates experience and which can be studied phenomenologically.

Within the psychoanalytic frame of reference there is a close correlation between the development of ego as a psychic structure and the experiencing of reality. The entire dynamic and developmental features of human personality growth are geared to the establishment of structures essential to experiencing reality, and the greatest source of fear and anxiety is related to loss of reality relationships and experiences of reality. Federn has postulated that the first step in the developmental processes of delineation and demarcation of the self is the establishment of the physical limits of the individual's body, i.e., the "bodily ego." He maintained that the existence of bodily feelings is essential in the formation of ego and the correlated experience of outer reality. "Corporal feeling" is seen as a progressive cathexis of the bodily boundaries with libidinal as well as destructive and self-preservative energies. In studying the phenomenon of estrangement, Federn indicated that such an experience may be understood not as a withdrawal of libido from external objects and an increase in narcissism by the ego, but rather as a reduction of cathexis of bodily boundaries, as a "loss of ego feeling." The delineation of bodily ego as a segment of reality involves a complex variety of sensory stimulations not related to any one area, structure or function of the body, but to the entire body as a whole. Lacking sufficient cathexis of his bodily boundaries, the individual does not possess the necessary psychological structures to experience himself as a reality separated and differentiated from others.

Of "ego feeling," the subjective aspect of ego boundary, Federn says, "Ego feeling is the sensation, constantly present, of one's own person, the ego's own perception of itself ... recognized objectively and ... constantly felt and perceived subjectively. We possess, in other words, an enduring feeling and knowledge that our ego is continuous and persistent ... because we feel that the processes within us ... have a persistent origin within us, and that our body and psyche belong permanently to our ego" (1952, pp. 60–1). This is obviously "ego feeling" as a dynamic and living entity, not merely as a theoretical abstraction.

The cardinal feature of "ego feeling" is not thought or knowledge but sensation. Federn adds, "A person senses where his ego ends, especially when the boundary has just changed" (p. 285). Slipping away of ego boundaries can be seen in the hypnogogic state as well as in the ideational experience of schizophrenics. The phenomenon is also observable in anesthesia, chemotherapies, anoxia, toxic states, chemical intoxications, and in the sensory reduction experiments of Hebb and others. In cases of cortical damage, there is also a loss of capacity to "experience distinction between oneself and the world" and a relative impairment in the capacity to maintain continuity of experience (Kaplan, 1964).

According to Federn (1952, p. 229), "The basis of sanity is correct and automatic recognition of (the) breach between subjective mental individual experiences and the world and the knowledge of the status of the world as it actually exists. Sanity means dealing with the world and with oneself with the facility of distinguishing clearly between them."

The ego and the sense of identity

The various adaptive processes mature and are integrated via the synthetic function into a nuclear, bodily ego interrelated with external reality. These processes contain skills and abilities characteristic of the individual, and the unique manner in which they are synthesized within the individual and infused with ego feeling leads to the development of the sense of identity.

Utilizing Federn's notion of "ego feeling," Erikson (1950) has attempted to trace the stages of ego development or maturation and integrate them with Freud's earlier delineation of psychosexual development. He indicates, on one hand, the various areas in which the sense of identity is built and, on the other, the manner in which an individual's culture and environment together channelize this development and, at the same time, set certain limits for it. DesLauriers (1962) and Freeman, Cameron, and

McGhie (1958), following Federn, have indicated that the *sine qua non* for the development of identity is the narcissistic cathexis of the bodily boundaries or the investment with "ego feeling" of these boundaries and the area circumscribed by them. An individual unable to distinguish the "me" from the "not-me" suffers from a severe loss of identity and experiences fusion of himself with other people and objects. This basic disturbance of "ego feeling" allows misconceptions of inner and outer happenings, precipitates hierarchical disorganization, and, hence, impairments of perception, hallucinations, delusions, and temporal discontinuities. Wherever there is reduced awareness of mental and bodily ego, thought processes may be experienced as divorced from control and, therefore, alien mechanisms. To these authors, "ego feeling," or the ability to differentiate self from the environment, is what is basically damaged in the schizophrenic reactions and leads to the loss of reality contact, loss of identity, and disorganization of mental processes. Once this is appreciated, schizophrenic "symptoms" can be viewed as necessary and understandable concomitants of malfunctioning.

DesLauriers points out that without sufficient narcissistic cathexis of the bodily boundaries, the individual is unable to maintain the necessary ego structures to experience himself as a reality separated and differentiated from others. Rather than simply withdrawing and creating a world of his own, the schizophrenic patient has lost the capacity to experience himself as integrated and real. His behavior can be understood then not as a defense against the threatening world or as an escape from unbearable experiences, but as disorganized, frantic efforts at discovering or re-discovering himself and establishing the bounds and limits of his reality, and ultimately creating the necessary conditions for a relationship to reality. The regaining of this relationship is the only condition that will permit integrated functioning and the resultant experience of stable identity. The model for the loss of boundaries, or the undifferentiated, unseparated state is, of course, the early experience of the neonate.

DesLauriers states that under these conditions, "Structurally the ego as a complex psychological organization ceases to exist so that the schizophrenic individual does not experience himself as a stable and reliable subject of his own experiences, and thus is incapable of experiencing a relationship to an object. Developmentally, the schizophrenic condition can be described as a regression, ... a dramatic representation of a level of behavior where the various psychological functions are undifferentiated, unintegrated, lacking goal directedness, and true reality value" (1962, pp. 51–2).

Summary of the theoretical evolution of the ego

Once it was appreciated that the ego was not merely the descriptive sum of executive functions nor the total of defenses mediating between id and reality, it was possible to conceptualize the ego's complex role in integrated personality functioning. Nunberg's concept of the synthetic function opened the way to understanding the manner in which the organism strived for greater economy of functioning via integration and differentiation of processes. Hartmann spelled out three distinct threads: id forces, primary autonomous ego functions, and conflictual defense buildup via the reality principle. He clarified the role of secondary processes as products of this interweaving, that is, secondary functions arising out of the matrix of integrated functioning and forming new amalgams of the individual's unique resources. Federn directly focused on the interweaving process to emphasize it as occurring in the context of relationship to reality and in the special context of the physical, delineated reality of the organism's body. This step led to understanding the structural linkage of the ego processes and reality, and the economics of the interdependence of intact, cathected ego psychological structures and the experience of reality. DesLauriers and Freeman, Cameron, and McGhie have separately developed structural models of schizophrenic disorganization on these theoretical bases. Their models postulate that the intactness of ego structures functioning in relationship to reality is required for a continuity of ego feeling and a sense of identity. In this framework the acutely schizophrenic person can be understood as having lost the capacity to experience himself as integrated and real; he is at the mercy of disorganization.

THE ONTOGENETIC DEVELOPMENT OF THE EGO

Having traced the major theoretical formulations regarding ego structure and function, it is important to focus more closely on how the ego develops. In this way we may be better able to detect differences between adequate and defective developmental patterns. In this presentation we adhere to certain assumptions. One of these is that psychological structure refers to enduring processes or functions, and we make no effort to translate these postulated structures from psychological to physical terms. A second assumption is that there is a mutual circular relationship between structure and experience. This is the concept that clarifies our understanding that structure influences interactions between organism and environment but also emphasizes that the nature of such interactions (as they are experienced by the organism) further modifies structure. Thus, a path is created which invites function; but as the path is established, its characteristics mold the traffic that will follow. A third assumption is one currently coming into acceptance in both psychoanalytic theory and academic psychology. This is that there is a primary ego function which strives for experience, challenge, mastery, and economy of functioning (White, 1959). We assume that this function is at the root of the individual's striving to achieve and maintain reality contact and to avoid the "psychological death" of a state of disorganization. Specifically, our assumptions regarding the ego can be outlined as follows:

(1) The ego is a hierarchy of successively more complex, highly differentiated and integrated organizations of

experience that provide for the personality a capacity to execute action, synthesize experience, and adapt to reality in a meaningful, gratifying manner.

(2) These executive, synthetic, and adaptive functions are possible only if the individual experiences himself as a unity separate and distinct from external reality; that is, only if the boundaries of his body are invested with "ego feeling."

(3) Ego development is a result of four factors:
   (a) the influences of the instinctual drives,
   (b) the influence of the environment,
   (c) the autonomous factors originating in hereditary material, and
   (d) the extent to which the experience of the previous three factors are integrated into the personality by the synthetic function of the ego.

(4) The quality and extent of impact of either environment or internal ego structures is a function of the synthetic function of the ego, that is, those characteristics of the ego that predispose it to invest "ego feeling" in the experience either of the self or of external reality.

(5) The structure of the ego is, in part, a function of the impact of the environment and, conversely, subsequent impact of the environment is a function of ego structures.

(6) Ego development is seen essentially as a process whereby the organism establishes hierarchical structures that organize experience, provide a frame of reference or a locus for those experiences which impinge upon it and wherein the sense of reality and the sense of identity are established. It is through these processes that the notion of personality becomes meaningful.

The emergence of a nuclear ego

Ego development is seen as proceeding successively through states which are not discrete, separate units of development, but rather as overlapping and interactive. At birth, it is evident that there is no stable frame of reference for the infant's inner experience. Even a rudimentary, primitive, kinesthetic self, or experiential "I" has not as yet appeared; the "me" and the "not-me" are undifferentiated. The neonate is a co-extensive with his world. Thus, to speak of "his" experience as confusion of ego and non-ego accompanied by felt omnipotence is to do an injustice to the undifferentiated, undefined, and amorphous quality of this experience.

A variety of experiential loci begin to develop. Their form is primitive and kinesthetic and they center around experiences of need satisfaction and sharp sensation. As the loci develop, some integration ensues as their experiential areas overlap. The unitary nature of the human body and its physical distinctiveness from the remainder of reality provide a basis for the infant's cumulative experiences of bodily limits as a global locus that begins to encompass and integrate an ever wider range of "pockets" or loci of experience. The raw, amorphous experiences become progressively differentiated into major loci of the "me" and the "not-me," the "inner" and "outer." Friction, the constraint of blankets, the coldness of wet diapers and the warmth of the mother's hand are examples of conditions that offer differential stimulation to the surface of the infant's body. These, in effect, not only provide opportunities for learning and experiencing the boundaries of the body but also establish an outline or framework for cumulative experiences of the boundaries of the "corporal" or bodily ego, the limits of the "me."

As this learning takes place, certain of the infant's experiences, bounded by the physical limits of this body, stand out in his perceptual field. A frame of reference for his experiences begins to develop. These experiences begin to be organized into an embryonic "me." The infant is no longer physically co-extensive with the world. His body becomes finite and limited and he can experience himself as an object in relationship to that which is not himself.

Once this nuclear core of self-experience has developed, secondary adaptive processes of the organism are synthesized into this core as they emerge. Functioning within a unitary framework fosters the organization of secondary processes within this context. Actually, the functions of perception, memory, and reality testing that Freud wrote of as primary processes fall into this category. Perception, as a complex process involving the maturation and differentiation of sensory mechanisms, motor systems and memory, becomes a means by which the total organism enters the act of relating to the immediate environment. Similarly, defensive operations become integrated systems of ego part processes as they develop in the context of the organism as a unit relating to external reality.

Concomitant with this process of synthesis is the process of differentiation. Those areas, functions and experiences that have been synthesized within the bodily boundaries also become more finely differentiated and specialized. The infant learns to respond differentially to the discomfort arising from an empty stomach and the discomfort arising from wet diapers. The sources of stimulation are experienced as separated and differentiated within space and within the context of his physical body. They function and are experienced not as isolated processes but as extensions or part functions of the unitary ego; they function as part of the total ego. As these processes of synthesis and differentiation continue, the infant's capacity to establish a frame of reference is enriched. The primary and secondary functions of the ego continue in their development. They are drawn into logical, coherent systems which are successively integrated and reintegrated at levels of greater complexity of organization.

While ego integration will always proceed as a product of experience, it is assumed that the integration of loci of experience into the crucial unit of self is a development which is not a maturational given, but a product of the convergence of complex psychological phenomena. As these phenomena gain their existence via the interaction between physical organism and external reality, integrations may even fail to form because prerequisite experiences are too impoverished or painful. The sequence and pattern of differentiation and integration may result in distorted (not reality bound) integrations matching peculiar distortions in the child's experience. At any rate, ego integration meshed with reality is a product of certain preconditions rather than an inevitability.

In the event that this critical development does not take place, the process of integration will become distorted. Adaptive functions, part processes, and primary and secondary autonomous functions can be present in a personality with distorted integration. However, such a personality will lack a logical, coherent organization and coordination based on a synchronized experience of reality and self. The ego crystallizes around reality because ego processes dealing with reality become reinforced and refined through experiences of interaction with reality. But if this development does not take place, some form of quasi- or pseudo-organization or fragmented functioning will develop and preempt a true synthesis of ego. Such developments take place because ego organization proceeds, but such developments are less adequate in coping with reality because they lack the logical, coherent, reality-based organization and the investment of ego feeling that makes for both a sense of identity and a sense of reality. Such developments are considered to be within this framework, vulnerable to disorganization, to form the basis of later schizophrenic function that will be discussed further.

The differentiation of the psychological ego

With the integration of ego functioning properly initiated, the organism must differentiate itself as a psychological being. The child is now able to pursue the learning of differentiation between his feelings, thoughts, actions, and external events. As he does this, he is able to establish his "mental" separateness from the world and his own distinction and identification.

It is at this stage that we see many evidences of primitive or magical thinking. The child still has not fully learned the parameters of reality in terms of logic and causality. Ego functions are not highly differentiated; the difference between wish and action is not clear; fantasies, thoughts and events are not well discriminated. Because of this lack of psychological distinctiveness, his feelings can be characterized as omnipotent or egocentric. He can become an imperious tyrant in a unilateral effort to bend the world to his will. When frustrated, he frequently lashes out in uncontrollable rage. His perception of events is restricted to a narrow perspective based on the concrete sensory data impinging upon him. The "theory of reality" with which he operates has narrow, restricted content and limited perspective.

Within the sphere of action, in its early less differentiated phase, we see a quality of imprinting or rote imitation. The child imitates the behavior of those about him, but is not quite clear about causes, relationships, and relevancies. Only later does action appear to be directed by the unified coordination of his own organism in response to its needs rather than as a part process reaction to the model of others around him.

As differentiation proceeds and the psychological self emerges, the obvious manifestations of egocentric thinking and feelings begin to drop away. More subtle forms remain, their disposition dependent upon the emerging strength of the ego and the opportunity of corrective, growth-producing experiences presented by the environment. It is obvious that even in seemingly mature adults some residuals of this quality of infantile experience generally remain.

Concomitant to the developing psychological separation of inner from outer experiences is the differentiation and organization of internal processes: thought, feelings, intention, will, and action are differentiated. Initially, feeling, fantasy, and act are globular and intermingled. To feel love is to express affection; to feel destructively disposed or to fantasy destruction is not clearly separated from destruction. Later, the child learns to categorize some acts as deliberate and hence within the realm of his responsibility, and others as "accidental" and for which he is blameless. Later, he is able to differentiate between thinking about, or wishing for something, and actually possessing it.

Perhaps the most significant event affecting this aspect of ego growth is the development of the capacity for conceptual symbolization. Previously, the child's experiences have been concretely kinesthetic and experiential in nature. Perceptual constancy and logical operations replace concrete, egocentric processes and are synthesized into the total psychic functioning as ego integration takes a rapid spurt. It becomes possible for the child to experience the "me" or self in a symbolic form. Experiences can now be condensed and given symbolic labels and a conceptual, cognitive memory becomes possible. Formal logical thought develops in terms of abstract concepts and causal relations.

As the differentiation of the bodily ego permitted the organism a physical experiential frame of reference, the differentiation and integration of the symbolic verbal and memory apparatuses provided the child with a basis for the integration of more complex experiences. He becomes capable of experiencing not just the concrete here and now, but can experience an enduring "self" in a time and space perspective. He can recall relevant past experiences without external cues and he can relate them to that which is expected at the moment; he can project a concept of himself into the anticipated future. Experiencing himself in temporal terms, he can begin to organize a set of percepts regarding that which is characteristic and enduring in him.

Social differentiation of the ego

Concomitant with the development of the psychological ego, the child begins to extend himself to relationships in the world about him. We observe evidence of this in the first primitive notions of ownership. Parents are "his" parents; toys are "his" toys; food is "his" food. The words "my" and "mine" begin to find their way into his vocabulary. Class and group identifications begin to form.

The development of an integrated self-percept is the prerequisite for the discovery of the child's relationship to other human beings about him. The child finds that others have thoughts, feelings, intentions, and actions similar or different from and contradictory to his own. He frequently finds that they can cause him pain and frustration, and they may permit his needs to go unmet. Because others can hurt and do so under given conditions, the child learns something about interaction and reciprocity. As he becomes acquainted with the fact that there are others who also experience and that frequently their experiences are similar to his, the capacity for empathy begins to develop. It appears probable that the greater the opportunity for the child at this stage to identify and empathize with widely varying individuals, the greater his capacity in adulthood to respect, tolerate, and empathize with individuals and groups different from himself.

This appreciation of others and their importance to the child is a basic requisite of ego development which precedes the learning of social standards and personal values. The child begins to experience and integrate such concepts as "right," "wrong," "good," "bad," "acceptable," "non-acceptable." A consistent pattern of behavior arises from the consistent framework of self-concept emerging from the child's psychological and social identities.

As the child grows, especially in latency and then adolescence, he integrates a perception of himself as a functional member of ever enlarging and more complex groups. He becomes a member of a family, of a sex, a race, a school, a community, and a culture. These memberships and his experience of them become woven into the functioning and the fabric of his ego. With the incorporation of each he takes on new social roles. The ego extends to those aspects of reality with which perhaps he has never had contact except in a symbolic way. He learns his relationship to a group that has had many years of history and tradition prior to his own existence.

VARIATIONS IN EGO DEVELOPMENT AND PSEUDO EGO DEVELOPMENT

Erikson's elaboration of Freud's psychosexual model pointed out how the economics of infantile sexuality could affect ego maturation. This approach helped give a systematic rationale to variations in character development. Erikson's model, however, is primarily interpersonally oriented — the modes that emerge in character are modes of the critical maturational events of early life and their relationship to the responsive environment of human caretakers. In the structural approach, we assume that there are similar influences on other aspects of ego development and that the qualities referred to by Rapaport as structural properties — thresholds of discharge, control systems, and integrative patternings — are vulnerable to influence and molding in various directions as a function of genetic material and experience. Unfortunately, the research and theory needed to support a systematic exposition of the range, qualities, and relationships involved in a thorough-going analysis of ego variations are still lacking.[1]

We need an Erikson to relate and systematize the work of Piaget and the child development theorists with that of the slowly evolving grasp of cognitive patterning (e.g., field-dependence — independence; leveling-sharpening, etc.).

In the absence of a systematic analysis we wish to present one form of ego variation that illustrates the implications of ego formation that does not follow the "normal" integrative pattern.

The constitutional givens of the human organism and the intrusive demands of physical reality are powerful forces fostering the creation of an adaptive integrated nuclear ego. However, as indicated above, the process is complex and intricate enough for this development to require an optimal range of conditions; beyond the range of these conditions an integrated nuclear ego cannot develop, although some form of adaptive development must occur if the organism is not to remain a helpless "vegetable." In the absence of the proper crystallization of the nuclear, reality-based ego, a variety of formations may occur which we shall refer to as "pseudo ego formations."

One can speculate about the possible conditions that foster pseudo ego development rather than that of true nuclear integration. These conditions may involve a quality of infantile experience which lacks proper richness, consistency or intensity for some constitutional reason. Or they may suffer these lacks because the particular child-environment (mother) interaction precludes the optimal experiences. These experiences may be not merely deficient, but they may be contradictory, inconsistent, or so dishar-

---

[1] To our knowledge, the thorough, systematic longitudinal work of Lois Murphy and her collaborators in the Menninger Foundation "Coping Project" comes closest to this goal.

monious that the infant cannot adequately integrate loci of experiences in the gradual development of hierarchical organization. The loci may be forced rather than harmoniously integrated into wider ranges of experience. At any rate, under these conditions ego integration and differentiation proceed not via synchronization with the solid anchor which reality provides but in a somewhat arbitrary pattern. Ego part processes can continue to mature, and the organism continues to strive for more economic functioning and for the gratifications that can come only via contact with reality. Consequently there is a tremendous impetus for "ego equivalent" integrations to emerge. We call this "pseudo ego integration" because the organization which develops lacks two essentials: it does not arise in the context of a base of experiences of a holistic organism bounded by the physical bodily limits and it does not arise out of an interplay between the organism as a unitary object in interaction with external reality.

The specific form of pseudo ego development that emerges depends on a range of factors similar to those responsible for normal ego growth. Constitutional variations, the parent-child interaction, and the cultural milieu all contribute. It is important to emphasize that we are not at this point talking about dynamics. The personality in the context of normal ego evolution develops internal conflicts, layerings of defenses, and various forms of functioning depending on shifts in psychic economics. But because of its harmonious integration, the normal ego does not easily fall prey to dangers of disruption of the ego processes. The normal ego does not have chronic or intermittent problems of maintaining structural integrity nor does it face the danger of losing reality orientation. In our case illustrations (Chapters V–VIII) there will be some evidence for the presence of dynamic conflicts in the patients even though the context will be that of basic ego dysfunction.

The cases will also give some idea of the possible range of pseudo ego patternings. With the exception of Mr. P, our sample reflects persons with pseudo ego (or ego defect) who have reached a point of intense ego disruption in their lives. Why this has occurred or why it has not yet occurred in Mr. P is a problem that does not yield to a ready generalization. Similarly, although we assume that Mr. B had a momentary phase of acute ego disorganization, he did not lapse into a more permanent state of such confusion. Why he did not but other patients did is also a problem not easily formulated in general terms. In each case, an understanding of the ego formation that does exist permits some hypotheses, just as examination of a normal ego permits assaying its pattern of functioning.

CHAPTER III

Structural Concepts in Test Analysis and Personality Description

The psychological evaluation emerges out of the psychologist's conceptions of three points: (a) his understanding of the tests and methods used and the functions they reflect, (b) his construction of the testee's perception of his task as well as the testee-tester interaction, and (c) the psychologist's definition of his function. This is to say that, in spite of the increased objectivity introduced by testing as opposed to less structured methods of assessment and the empirical foundations of the tests, the psychologist remains the most important "instrument" in the evaluation. Since there is no direct correspondence between scores on given tests and certain patient characteristics in which one might be interested (e.g., organicity, psychosis, depression), the psychologist retains the task of arriving at a description of the patient which will permit conceptualization of the patient's total personality organization and functioning which may, in turn, yield the end product: predictions to non-test behavior. His integrations of the data emerging from the testing situation become the mediating constructs — patient behavior and test data are on one side, extrapolation to extra-test behavior are on the other. Thus, the psychologist's capacity for appropriate and relevant synthesis of data is a key factor in test usage. If the goals of clinical psychological evaluation set down in Chapter I (i.e., greater understanding of the patient and relevance of understanding to treatment) are to be realized, the psychologist must bring to the situation a theoretical approach adequate to carry out this task.

The role which the psychologist sees himself as serving determines to a large extent how he will function. His goals bear on his perception of the nature of testing, on the selection of tests which he employs, the types of concepts he uses in deriving information from the psychological examination, and the ways in which he communicates with his colleagues. The psychologist's task and goals are closely related to the kind of setting in which he works, what it offers, and the clientele it serves. For the purpose of description, let us consider a range of situations posing different kinds of diagnostic problems. At one end of this range the psychologist may work with a client population in the position of matching the abilities and liabilities of individuals with various job opportunities. In this case, he is generally safe in assuming that his clients are relatively intact in more basic personality characteristics of internal equilibrium and personality integration. Rather, he is concerned with matching client variables such as work habits, interest areas, conceptual adequacy, and capacity to relate cooperatively with occupational requirements.

At a second step, the psychologist may predominantly encounter a population that seeks professional service for symptoms of personal discomfort and interpersonal problems. These people usually have a "niche" in society and do not behave in any way that forces restraining or protective action from others. At this level, the psychologist generally utilizes a conceptual framework that is focused on the dynamics of psychic functioning such as internal conflicts, defenses, characterological developments, symbolic communication of unconscious processes, perception of others, and modes of interpersonal relationships.

At a third step of this range, the psychologist may encounter persons who have engaged in certain maladaptive behavior and have come to the attention of authorities in any one of a number of situations. Problems of impulsive action, sexual behavior, criminal acts, addictions, etc., may be included in a much longer list of difficulties. At this level, the psychological examination is geared relatively more in the direction of differential diagnosis in terms of basic character development, general style of coping, and patterns of motivation and energy utilization.

At the fourth step, at the end of the continuum, the psychologist will encounter patients who have temporarily or chronically experienced a breakdown. or impairment in adaptive capacity. His concerns will be directed toward understanding the causes of such disruption with a view to implementing differential treatment programs depending upon his understanding of the source of impairment or defect. He will seek knowledge of the individual's capacity for internal integration and ability to maintain reality contact. Hence, the psychologist shifts his focus and his conceptualizations in accordance with the nature of the patient's functioning. This does not mean that a single level of analysis is automatically given depending on the presenting problem, but it does indicate that the kinds of concepts used and the kinds of data sought will vary depending on the level of personality functioning considered to be relevant.

The interaction between the patient and the examiner is no less important than the psychologist's definition of his task. Regardless of the level of problem to be evaluated or the psychologist's perception of his professional role in a given setting, the testing situation involves two people who retain their unique human characteristics. Schachtel (1943), among others, has described the relevance of the test "posture" assumed by the patient. Patients define the test situation, consciously or unconsciously, according to their own needs, wishes, and fears. Distortions may be introduced by the various manifestations of different authoritarian orientations and can be seen or inferred in the testee's dealings with the tester and the test. Schachtel has described the influence of such attitudes as attempting to please, following the rules to the letter, demonstrating prowess either quantitatively or qualitatively, being afraid of being "found out," resenting the intrusion into one's privacy, or manifesting an aura of indifference. Schachtel also observes that people who take the test seriously are the people who take other situations seriously, but there are differences among personality types in the way they take it seriously; e.g., the pedant's interpretation of the situation is not the same as that of the anxious or melancholic patient.

Schachtel's observation that patients transfer the attitudes, needs, fears, wishes, defenses, strivings, and interests characteristic of other situations in life to the test situation might also be applied to testers. Schafer (1954) has dealt with this concept in detail in his discussion of tester-testee interaction and the relationship of tester personality variables to demands made, implicitly or explicitly, on the patient. Both Schachtel and Schafer remind us that the test responses themselves and the patient's test attitudes and behavior confirm, amend, and amplify one another, and all of this is important in the inference process. The authors would emphasize this point relative to the tester's subjective responses to the patient. Instead of being irrelevant or detrimental, the tester's feelings and reactions are important data for hypothesis development. While it is important to be aware of one's affective reactions in order to control bias, it is also useful to determine the emotional impact that the patient may have on another person. For example, the irritation felt by an examiner can often lead to his understanding of very subtle passive-aggressive techniques used by a patient. Again, a vague discomfort can often lead the psychologist to review a portion of the patient's behavior and may reveal a peculiar flaw in logic or reasoning or a disguised misperception. The examiner can also be alert to such questions as: how a particular patient was able to appear to behave adequately in the interpersonal situation and yet appear extremely disturbed on the tests; what about the patient's way of dealing with the situation evoked particular feelings in the tester?

Essentially, the point is that the examiner draws data from a wide range of behavior and by subjecting these to relevant theoretical scrutiny he brings them under control so that they can make a contribution to a valid personality representation.

STRUCTURAL CONCEPTS AND THEIR
RELATIONSHIP TO TEST BEHAVIOR

As described in Chapter II, structural concepts refer to the means of integration and organization of ego functioning and to the subsequent styles or patterning of such functioning. This process or set of subprocesses has concomitants in three main areas: in one area of functioning, the ego part processes or internal processes are brought into concert or integration; in the second area, higher ego processes develop which regulate the interaction of an integrated ego system in relationship to the external environment; the third major function forms the basis of the person's experience as an integral, discrete being continuing his existence in time and space, which may be described as the phenomenological function. Each of these facets of ego function-ing can be examined more closely with a view toward developing its test behavior concomitants.

The ego serves a range of functions that are variously called into service depending on the momentary demands being made upon it. In terms of the ego functions outlined in Chapter II, we conceive of the ego as always in some state of activation and in relationship or attempted relationship to reality. The test battery provides a pre-planned set of conditions for the individual to deal with and the conditions are so designed as to impose varying demands. It is, of course, impossible to draw a sample directly from the various situations in real life to which each subject is exposed or likely to be exposed. On the other hand, even if it were feasible to take video tape samples of our patients under various condi-tions and subject these to micro-analysis, we still would fall short of the range of conditions afforded in our usual test battery. Because the tests artificially contrive problem situations, the range of functioning which they tap is potentially broader than that which could be obtained by an analysis of a cross-section of a person's current adaptive behavior to more "real" conditions. In real life, the ambiguity or lack of directiveness that can be structured in tests cannot be obtained outside of prolonged and extreme laboratory conditions. However, tests can create conditions which approach or equal the diffuseness or lack of clarity which occur when a patient suffers some degree of ego impairment. In other words, tests go beyond the range of current environmental stress and present the patient with conditions that he may encounter when some of his own ego functions are impaired. Thus, our view is that tests tap the adaptive functioning of the ego by imposing demands, dilemmas, and challenges of various types and sufficient range to assess its structure.

EGO DEMANDS AND TEST DIMENSIONS

The general paradigm of the test situation involves the examiner presenting a problem situation; the patient is required to engage in processes of perception and/or cognition to interpret the task and provide for himself the information needed to determine the nature of an appropriate response. The patient must engage in psychological functioning by drawing on his resources to gather relevant data; he must organize what is available to him with a view toward developing a response that he considers to be appropriate (or adaptive) behavior, and he must then engage in a process of communication conveying the product of these maneuvers to the waiting examiner.

The testee is in an interpersonal situation in the role of patient in a professional setting. The situation is charged with personal meaning; it draws attitudes and feelings regarding the person's concept of who he is and elicits profound motivational forces. In this sense the psychological examination is like a biopsy. A small segment of tissue is removed but that small segment is unquestionably a sample or representation of the remaining tissue. The patient's test behavior is a sample of his modes, capacities, and styles of adaptive functioning.

The goal of the structural approach is to derive a picture of the individual's ego in operation, i.e., the functioning of the part processes and of the synthetic function. The psychologist's ability to construct a truly representative picture of such functioning is contingent upon presenting the patient with a wide representative range of demands and, therefore, it is essential to use an appropriate battery of tests and to include a clinical interview in the evaluation. In practice, it is important that the psychologist maintain essentially the same tests in the same order so that he develops a consistent baseline of prior experiences for comparison purposes that would be lacking if continual experimentation with test order were employed. Certainly, circumstances may dictate flexibility in the instruments utilized and in their presented order but, whenever there is freedom of choice, standardization of procedure is desirable.

The more usual theory of projective testing postulates that the less structured tests in a battery provide the subject with an opportunity to respond in terms of his own needs, drives, conflicts, and defensive or coping style. The structural approach broadens the range of test situations in which elements of individual styles are considered and thus includes intelligence testing as well as tests which involve psychomotor skill (e.g., the Bender-Gestalt). The basic battery utilized by the authors includes one of the Wechsler intelligence tests (formerly the Wechsler-Bellevue I, now the Wechsler Adult Intelligence Scale), the Rorschach, the BRL Sorting Test, the Story Recall Test, the Bender-Gestalt, the Thematic Apperception Test, and a Clinical Interview. Additional testing instruments may be employed for special purposes.

Because these instruments, when administered as a battery, vary in terms of clear directionality and hence in the demands made upon the ego, they provide a matrix of information about the person undergoing evaluation. The dimension of directionality as applied to the tests refers to the nature of the cues inherent in the tests themselves and the instructions that accompany the test material in regard to what is expected of the individual. There is a continuum in a test battery ranging from those tasks that contain few clues as to how the patient is to perform to those which possess a great deal of information about how one is to operate in the task and what manner of response is called for. The dimension of directionality has frequently been referred to as one of test structure. While this is a meaningful term, we must clarify the difference between the terms "test structure" and "personality structure." Personality or ego structure in our usage refers to the kind of or quality of organizational capacity, the manner in which the ego part processes achieve integration, the manner in which energy is bound and utilized, and the style of adaptive framework. Test structure is the quality of information-giving intrinsic to the nature of a task presented to the subject. Test structure may more specifically be conceptualized in terms of the interaction of the two dimensions of (1) goal clarity-ambiguity and (2) stimulus clarity-ambiguity. The dimension of goal clarity-ambiguity has reference to the properties of the task which define the nature of the subject's expected behavior. In a test with relatively greater goal clarity, the expected behavior (goal or end product) is relatively clear, explicitly stated, or implicitly delimited within a certain range. The situation may have built-in "feedback" or "control of error," meaning that responses themselves give evidence of "fitting" or "not fitting." Or the situation may give "information" in the sense of directing the subject to a specified area of consideration. For example, a Block Design item of the Wechsler Adult Intelligence Scale (WAIS) carries possibilities of feedback because attempted solutions can be immediately checked against the picture model; the Information subtest has a high degree of "clarity" in that an item tells the subject what kind of an answer is required (e.g., "How *far* is it from Paris to New York?"). The WAIS, Bender-Gestalt, Memory Scale, and Figure Drawing Tests are high in goal clarity.

Goal ambiguity implies the other end of this continuum: the expected behavior is not explicitly stated; there is a relatively wide range of responses which will satisfy task demands; goal direction is relatively broad and a circumscribed range of thought is not intrinsic to the task. Consequently, the testee is left to choose his own range; he has to determine what he will accomplish and what he will consider a legitimate end product. Hence, he must impose relatively more of his own initiative, discretion, resources, and judgment. Certainly the Rorschach is a test which is low on the dimension of goal clarity (or high on goal ambiguity) since, "What might this be?" does not tell the testee what to see, that is, does not steer his functioning in any direction other than that of a percept in the visual modality and one having some manner of relationship to the visual stimulus in front of him. Similarly, some Wechsler items leave the end product relatively ambiguous, e.g., those in the Comprehension subtest require some degree of judgment to give an appropriate reply. Considering whole tests in the battery, the BRL Sorting Test and the TAT, in addition to the Rorschach, can be placed in the category of having high goal ambiguity.

The stimuli provided by the test may be seen as the "tools" or "ingredients" used by the testee in fulfilling the task or reaching an explicit or implicit goal. Thus, the second dimension, that of stimulus clarity-ambiguity, refers to the nature of these tools or ingredients. High stimulus clarity can be defined in terms of the subject's being given relatively definite tools to use and told how to use them. The stimuli may lend themselves to a relatively limited number of interpretations. In the case of Block Design, the ingredients are quite literally building blocks; the testee does not have to cast about to determine with what to make the designs.

Fig. 1
Location of Tests on the Dimensions of
Goal Clarity-Ambiguity and Stimulus
Clarity-Ambiguity

II Figure Drawings	goal clarity	I Wechsler Bender-Gestalt Memory Scale
stimulus ambiguity		stimulus clarity
III Rorschach	goal ambiguity	IV Sorting Test TAT

Similarly, in the Sorting Test, the examiner asks the subject to do something with *these* objects and the material to be employed stops with the thirty-three items offered. However, it is not merely the delimited or circumscribed nature of the stimuli that is being considered in this dimension but that of clarity or obvious meaningfulness of the stimuli. In this sense, the TAT is also a test with clear stimuli except for a few cards and a few details on some of the cards. Generally, the TAT pictures do not require an act of interpretation of what is there; they are not abstract art. It is only when the task of what the subject must do with the stimuli is introduced that the challenge of interpretation is encountered. Other tests falling into the category of high stimulus clarity are the WAIS, Bender-Gestalt, and Memory Scale, in addition to the Sorting Test and TAT.

In the case of high stimulus ambiguity, the stimuli themselves have little or no intrinsic organization; there is a wide range of possible interpretations or conceptualizations of the stimuli, and the subject is to a greater extent left on his own to decide what data to utilize, what inner resources to relate, how to organize and formulate his responses, how to judge what is more or less

Fig. 2
Ego Functions Demanded by Various Combinations of
Task and Stimulus Conditions

II	I
(1) recognition of task demands and following directions	(1) recognition of task demands and following directions
(2) formulation of the means by which to reach the goal	(2) recognition and use of appropriate limited response area
(3) checking performance against goal demands and reality considerations	(3) drawing on past learning, memory, "everyday" problem solving modes
(4) perceptual-motor coordination	(4) attention, concentration, reflectivity, judgment, logical reasoning in circumscribed areas
	(5) logical, coherent communication
	(6) perceptual-motor coordination

goal clarity (between columns II and I)

stimulus ambiguity   stimulus clarity

III	IV
(1) imposing goal direction	(1) imposing goal direction
(2) formulation of means to end product	(2) circumscribing thought range-appropriate judgment of how far to go from stimuli and still satisfy implicit task demands
(3) capacity for drawing on past and present experience, relaxing some of the usual controls on thought processes, making new associations and integrations	(3) perception and interpretation of relevancy of response: judgment of quality
(4) perception and interpretation of relevancy of response	(4) logical organization and connections imposed on stimuli and response
(5) organization of response	(5) logical and coherent communication
(6) presentation of ideas, percepts with a sense of appropriateness to the implied demands of reality-situation and goal	
(7) judgment of quality of response	
(8) logical, coherent communication	

goal ambiguity (between columns III and IV)

acceptable use of the tools. The Figure Drawings and Rorschach Test are seen as providing ambiguous materials.

THE TWO-DIMENSIONAL MATRIX
AS A HEURISTIC MODEL

Although these two dimensions — goal clarity and stimulus clarity — may not be strictly orthogonal, it appears that the tests in the clinical battery can be schematically located in terms of where they fall on these dimensions, as illustrated in Figure 1. It must be remembered that within any given test, subtests will also vary along these dimensions. However, such a classification has descriptive and heuristic value in that major test characteristics and functional demands on the testee may be more precisely identified. It is apparent that a main factor in test structure runs diagonally through quadrants I and III of the matrix of Figure 1. Here we find the traditional axis of "test structure" with the "objective" tests (Wechsler, Bender-Gestalt, etc.) in quadrant I and the Rorschach in quadrant III. However, we gain clearer perspective of the properties of the Sorting Test by not placing it somewhere median along the same axis, but in quadrant IV where it is located by the combination of stimulus clarity and goal ambiguity. The TAT and the Figure Drawings give us more difficulty. As indicated above, the stimulus qualities of the TAT indicate this test to be on the stimulus clarity side; however, the task of finding an appropriate goal and determining the adequacy of the end product places this test on the ambiguity side of the goal dimension. The Figure Drawings are the inverse; the end product is specified (although still leaving some range of choice) but no ingredients are offered. The interview, an integral part of the battery, may fall into any of the four quadrants dependent upon how it is structured by the interviewer. Indeed, the examiner can use the interview to provide additional data in any quadrant (along any combination of dimensions) where, in a given examination, other test data are felt to be lacking or incomplete.

Further heuristic value of this matrix lies in the possibility of delineating fairly discrete ego functions or combinations of ego functions for each quadrant. In our experience, the matrix is useful to students because it forcefully directs attention to concepts of ego functioning and fosters a perspective of the overall patterning gained from the range of data in the test battery. In quadrant I, the functions appear to be those that obtain in relatively structured "everyday" situations where the patient may have the support of ready recognition of the relationships of current demands to past experiences with relatively less necessity for recourse to "rethinking," reanalyzing, or introducing the mediating effects of personal judgment.

In quadrants II and IV, the subject encounters another quality of task — one which is not remote from everyday experience but which requires much from the subject in the way of resourcefulness, logical organization, maintenance of continuing effort, and appropriate relating of conclusions or end product to the situational givens. Since in quadrant II the goal is specified and in quadrant IV the tools are given, the ego stress of tasks in these quadrants is of an intermediate nature, demanding more from the subject's response repertoire than the utilization of possibly over-learned behaviors (as in quadrant I) but less than the demand on resources commonly associated with the "regression in the service of the ego" of quadrant III. It is in quadrant III that the most severe stress is placed upon the ego in that the most difficult task in real life or in a testing situation is one which requires the individual to create meaningfulness and muster his own goals, tools or ingredients, methods of approach, and criteria for evaluation. The tasks of quadrant III demand a relatively abstract or "as if" attitude coupled with the need for integration of the cognitive processes of perception, association, and concept formation, (as well as attention, concentration, and anticipation), all applied to the intermingling of imaginative free fantasy and responsible reality testing. Potentialities for ego weakness or deficit as well as adaptive problem solving will generally be more clearly observed in quadrant III tasks, whereas the tasks of the other three quadrants will illuminate the relative contributions of these ego characteristics to more ordinary but qualitatively different situations. In patients whose ego impairment is more acute, evidence of impaired functioning will be more manifest in areas II and IV and even, in severe impairment, in area I.

Figure 2 lists the functions that appear to be involved in the various combinations of test conditions. The model demonstrates the interplay between environmental conditions and ego functions called forth. These are precisely the kind of data required to give an appraisal of ego variables; these data can be generalized to extra-test variables, especially those having therapeutic potential.

INDIVIDUAL INSTRUMENTS AND STRUCTURAL APPRAISAL

The validity of the psychologist's final understanding and integration of the patient's functioning is intimately related to his having obtained the patient's responses to a sufficiently wide range of demands. Where there is overlap in functions tapped by the separate tests, the psychologist has points of comparison for judging the reliability of his observations. The rationale for the choice of instruments used by the authors is based upon the assumptions made about the functions tapped by each instrument. These assumptions are presented in the following discussion.

The Wechsler Adult Intelligence Scale (WAIS)

As noted above, the WAIS is a test of relatively high directionality and low ambiguity. However, among the subtests there is a degree of variation in these dimensions. This aspect enriches the Wechsler as a test of ego functioning in that comparisons can be made of the patient's ability to deal with the varying demands posed by the subtests, in addition to information gained about the patient's intellectual functioning. Some subtests of the WAIS are relatively clear in what they require. For example, in the Information subtest, the instructions are explicit; the area of ego functioning tested is a narrow segment of implementation of past learning and memory with a minimum of judgment and organization required. However, the Comprehension subtest represents somewhat less clarity or directionality. Answers here must meet certain logical requirements posed by the questions, but there is less intrinsic directiveness as to the nature of the answers. The patient's answers depend on an element of judgment which he brings to bear relevant to what the questions implicitly rather than explicitly demand of him. He must recognize that the test item really says, "What do you think is the 'proper' answer to give a psychologist asking this question in the midst of a psychological examination?"

The ego functions tapped by the various subtests are complex and cannot be reduced to easily defined unitary or pure part processes. Likewise, tests which require or do not require synthetic functioning cannot be specified definitively since synthetic functioning may be involved in the subject's mode of dealing with any of the tasks and a breakdown in synthetic functioning will affect the part processes being used. However, following Rapaport's thinking, the authors assume that the more prominent ego demands can be identified for each subtest in addition to the differential stress imposed by varying degree of structure.[1]

The *Information & Vocabulary* subtests involve past learning and memory — the capacity for storing and retrieving verbal information, intellectual alertness, and awareness of the world and, to some extent, facility in using language.

Comprehension, as mentioned, taps reasoning and judgmental capacity. The subject, to perform adequately, must have some

[1]Rapaport, D., Gill, M.M., & Schafer, R., *Diagnostic Psychological Testing,* Year Book, Chicago, 1945, or Holt's new edition, International Universities Press, New York, 1968.

perspective on the issues involved, must "center-in" on the crucial issue of each question while maintaining enough psychological distance to avoid becoming personally and emotionally entangled, and must organize a meaningful communication for the examiner.

Picture Arrangement asks the subject to demonstrate a certain amount of social judgment and capacity for recognizing social nuances as well as requiring logical organization and planning ability. It is good practice to ask the patient to explain the stories in that he may have missed or distorted the usually acceptable theme even though the cards are placed in an acceptable sequence.

Digit Span demands a capacity for attention and immediate recall and hence is susceptible to impairment by anxiety, preoccupation, and distractibility. *Arithmetic,* in addition to computational ability, requires attention, concentration, logical organization, and utilization of available "free energy." *Digit Symbol,* in addition to attention and concentration, requires visual-motor facility. Because of their requirements for concentration, Digit Span, Arithmetic, and Digit Symbol are all highly sensitive to the effects of anxiety and fluctuation of attention.

Picture Completion is a measure of critical reasoning; it asks the subject to identify the essential missing detail in a perceptual task in terms of what most people would consider essential. It is also a measure of the capacity to scrutinize visual perceptual data in a critical manner — a measure of what is currently referred to as "field independence."

Block Design appears to require abstract-conceptual thinking as well as visual-motor coordination. It requires analysis and synthesis, the recognition of part-whole relationships. *Object Assembly,* likewise, involves visual-motor organization and a recognition of part-whole relationships. On both of these subtests the examiner may see indications of the patient's capacity for balancing a systematic approach to problem solving and flexible trial and error. These qualities can also be seen as ingredients in the dimension of field independence. Motility, frustration tolerance, and control factors may also be identified. Anxiety, depression, and synthetic function impairment may interfere with adequate performance.

The *Similarities* subtest implicitly demands verbal, abstract-conceptual ability. The subject must consider a range of possibilities and come through with an answer of "best fit." From the responses, the examiner may see how the subject orders the "scheme of things" and the level of relating them, i.e., concrete, functional, conceptual, or otherwise. The Similarities subtest and the Sorting Test are both measures of concept formation and can be profitably compared for insights into the patient's thinking and reasoning processes.

The WAIS in general reflects the patient's ability to deal with relatively structured, "everyday" situations. As the patient deals with the tasks, the examiner has information about the functioning of part processes, synthetic ability, interference by anxiety, effects of depression, and indications of thought disorder or ego defects of other types. It is important to differentiate between temporary inefficiencies and more basic impairments. Certainly, stylistic variables (e.g., hysteric, obsessive-compulsive) and dynamic components are also reflected. As on all tests, the examiner must be an astute and careful observer and recorder since all behavior is subject to the inference process.

The Sorting Test

The Sorting Test, described by Rapaport *et al.,* has not been widely used except by Topeka-trained psychologists although the publication of a new edition of Rapaport's *Diagnostic Psychological Testing* may have a stimulating effect. Because we consider it so useful, a manual for the use of the Sorting Test is included as an appendix to the present publication.[2] The test consists of thirty-three common objects (e.g., a red rubber ball, silverware, tools, bicycle bell, etc.). The stimuli as such do not require interpretation, but the test does require the patient to impose order, system, and organization according to his ability to judge appropriateness. The two parts of the test present complementary ego demands in terms of the dimension of test directionality. In the second portion, labeled the passive part, the task is one of recognizing the scheme of organization that the examiner has imposed by a given selection of items. This requires recourse to a repertoire of conceptual possibilities that the patient selects and judges for appropriateness. In the active part, administered first, the task is the more difficult one of creating a selection of items that will constitute a piece of organization, but there are no cues given that tell the person how to select an organization base. The ego has to work harder because the environment provides less direction: the person is more dependent on his own ego resources in the process of determining what possible solutions will fit the requirements of consensual reality and in selecting, screening, and judging what may be a "good" answer. In either part, the patient must use concepts that have relevance in the particular context, that recognize dominant properties of the available objects, have "face" validity, and can be communicated logically.

From the patient's manner of dealing with the Sorting Test, one may draw data regarding the capacity for and utilization of abstract-conceptual thinking as well as evidence of illogical, irrelevant, or "loose" (poorly integrated) thinking. This instrument is generally more sensitive than the Wechsler Similarities subtest in detecting disorders in abstraction, probably because the ordering of objects demands more active participation in the determination of the proper level of conceptualization and the ego does not have recourse to overlearned verbal responses. In general, disturbance on

---

[2] In addition to the appendix to this volume, see also Appendix B of Colarelli, N.J. & Siegel, S.M., *Ward H.* for a quantitative scoring system for the Sorting Test.

the active part has relatively less serious implications than pathology evident from behavior on the passive section due to the difference in test structure. For example, a "well-preserved" paranoid may have great difficulty with the active part because he has few cues to guide him toward appropriate responses. This same person may do very well on the passive part because enough structure is provided for him to "shore up" his basic deficit in reality testing. If he has difficulty on both portions, his paranoid adaptive functioning is critically impaired.

The Bender-Gestalt

The Bender-Gestalt Test is given and used by the authors in a manner somewhat different from the traditional way and as a supplementary test rather than a major instrument. It is administered three times. Initially, in the "five-second" Bender, the cards are presented one at a time for five seconds each, and the subject is asked to observe the card during the five-second exposure and to draw the design as soon as each card is removed. Second, the "copy" Bender is presented in the standard fashion: the patient is asked to copy each design directly from the original card as accurately as he can and to go on to the next card when he is ready. In the final administration, the "memory" Bender involves asking the subject to draw from memory as many of the figures as he can recall. The task requires attention, perception, memory, and visual-motor coordination. Such functioning is vulnerable to impairment seen in organic damage, ego impairment, mental retardation, and minimal motivation.

Human Figure Drawings

The Figure Drawings are also used as a supplementary test. The testee is first asked to draw a person, then a person of the opposite sex, and lastly, himself. The most basic structural use to be made of this task is the observation of how the testee deals with this rather simple and yet somewhat ambiguous demand with the assumption that there is a parallel between the way the patient deals with extra-test reality and the way he handles the reality of this task.

The goal or expected end product of this exercise is stated rather directly and concretely ("Draw a picture of a person"), but the means to that end must come from the individual being evaluated. The patient must determine what sort of person he will draw from a number of possibilities (sex, age, position, dress, expression, etc.) and formulate how such a person can be represented in terms of physical attributes, proportions, unique identifying characteristics, and the like. The process appears to be one of formulation and implementation through a series of successive approximations in which the testee uses data from his perception of reality to determine what he must do and how he evaluates and modifies the emerging product; the feedback that he derives from his emerging drawing provides a basis for modification in an intentional direction and in the light of reality considerations. Where there are ego malfunctions, the patient is less capable of undistorted perception, and drawings may show breaks in the body wall, transparencies, distortions, grossly disproportionate relationships among parts, disturbances in space, peculiar postures, emptiness within the figure, and related phenomena which indicate impairment in reality testing. The patient's reaction to his drawings illustrates a general principle of self-evaluation applicable to all of the tests. The manner in which the patient carries out the task and reacts to his own production yields data regarding where the patient may be placed on a continuum of (1) can do the task and knows he can, to (2) cannot accomplish the task but is able to see where his performance falls short, thus revealing that certain critical functions of reality testing are intact, to (3) cannot do the task and is not capable of critical appraisal. While this tripartite distinction is oversimplified, the clinician should be aware of the differential implications. Ego functions are more impaired and treatment requirements are different when the patient has little or no awareness of the gap between his current functioning and what would be his more adequate functioning under other conditions.

The authors are aware that some psychologists assume that there is isomorphism between the drawn figure and the individual's body image and also between certain aspects of the figure and the patient's dynamic problems. We question the first theoretical proposition in that patients with ego disturbance do not have the functioning ability to perceive themselves or their drawings consistently and without distortion. It seems reasonable to assume that the observed relationship between the distorted figure drawings produced by patients with poor ego functioning and their impaired body images stem from a common source, the ego defect. In the case of ego malfunction the second assumption is questioned for the same reason. For patients with more intact egos, dynamic problems may be given precedence in the process of inference since the drawing of a human figure may arouse anxieties and conflicts, and prompt defensive reactions. For patients with ego defects, dynamics are involved but the ease of developing inferences of this type should not overshadow concern with ego problems and their nature. Again, we would reiterate the point that dynamic considerations must be seen within the context of how the ego functions.

The Rorschach Test

Relative to the other instruments in the test battery, the Rorschach represents the least directional clarity and the highest level of stimulus ambiguity (see Fig. 1). Not only does the test avoid telling the patient what kinds of percepts to develop but it fails to provide specific ingredients or delineated tools. The blots are to be used, but unless the patient is to reply that they are blots, that they are symmetric, or spotty, or colored in a particular manner, he must use his own inner resources to create something more than a report of the manifest stimuli offered on the cards. In this task the patient "projects" in the sense of offering creations that reflect inner ideational and emotional predispositions. However, at a structural level, he is also engaged in a difficult ego maneuver in that he must impose goal direction on his efforts, integrate his resources with the stimuli, formulate and screen his responses in terms of what he judges to be appropriate and acceptable, and communicate his formulation to the examiner. In other words, he must permit his mind to range beyond the "givens" and give some degree of liberty to ideational and emotional associations. This requires a relaxation of secondary processes, although the elements that the patient produces must then be reincorporated into secondary process thinking as the task proceeds to the requirements of producing an integrated percept that meets the implicit demands of acceptability. This is the concept of "regression in the service of the ego." The phrase "service of the ego" is critical because it emphasizes the organization and adaptive components that compliment the "regression" components.

The lack of structure in the Rorschach Test makes it difficult for the patient to avoid revealing his resources and limitations. Where the responses are restrictive, they give information about inhibition or limitation of "regressive" capacity or of the defensive control of "regressive" phenomena. Where percepts reflect a freer responsiveness of associations beyond the immediately given stimulus properties, the responses can be analyzed to indicate the quality of resourcefulness and resiliency or the degree to which the associated elements "break free" of the patient's capacity to modulate them within an organized framework.

No attempt will be made here to discuss the various stylistic and dynamic data which are manifested and add to the total picture of patient functioning. Schafer (1954) has nicely covered this area in detail with respect to neurotic functioning. Structurally, we are concerned with the patient's responses as indices of his internal integration and synchronization with reality. The "acceptable" response is judged as such in terms of consensual reality (certain kinds of responses are conceivable by most people and other responses most people would not find conceivable) and "goodness of fit," or form level. The psychologist is evaluating ego functioning when he makes inferences about the patient's capacity to deal with internal and external stimuli in a creative and integrative way, in a fragmented or undifferentiated manner, or in a manner which suggests a gross breakdown in synthetic function as seen in fabulized combinations, confabulations, and certain overt symbolic representations. Ego functioning is also involved in the patient's capacity, as inferred from the Rorschach, to modulate affect and impulse, to deal meaningfully with inclusive or partial segments of his perceptual world, to bring to bear a relative richness or barrenness of "mental content," and to impose logical and communicable structure upon the more ambiguous facets of his perceptual field. The reader may recognize that those positive, strength-connoting statements above may be subsumed under the concept of secondary autonomy, the opposite end of the continuum from ego impairment. The concept of secondary autonomy has been discussed in Chapter II and refers to a multi-dimensional concept, as suggested by Banta (1970), who defines autonomy as ". . . self-regulating behaviors that facilitate effective problem solving." Implied in this definition and further expanded by Banta is the idea that autonomous functioning is reality-syntonic, i.e., it enables adaptation to the demands of everyday living, but it is centrally motivated, self-regulated behavior which gives the individual freedom to use responses appropriate to the situation (such as dependence or independence) and the freedom to innovate, i.e., to find alternative and unique ways of thinking and acting since conventional behaviors are not always the most adaptive ones. Three general factors may be considered to be involved in autonomy: (1) receptivity, or the capacity to feel curiosity and thus to manipulate, to explore, and to experience oneself and the world, and to flexibly change one's orientation to ideas and objects; (2) reflectivity, or the capacity to inhibit impulsive behavior when the task demands it; and (3) creativity, or the capacity to innovate, to bring ideas into new combinations and associations and give rise to a product which is socially communicable, meets certain specified requirements, or is in some way useful. In a broad sense the psychologist uses the entire clinical battery to evaluate ego autonomy and, to the extent that the patient cannot function autonomously, one is able to grasp the extent and nature of pathology. Among the tests comprising the battery, however, the Rorschach places the greatest demands upon those factors which, when synthesized, enable self-regulated behavior. Thus, the Rorschach gives the greatest insight into the autonomous functioning or impairment of the patient's ego.

The Thematic Apperception Test

The TAT has been used extensively as a key to dynamics and as revealing aspects of self-perception and perception of one's environment. The importance of stylistic and structural aspects must also be emphasized. The degree to which the patient gives imaginational and affective components to his stories indicates his capacity and freedom to involve such aspects in his mental life. The patient's style of coping or control may be revealed in his thought organization, the extent to which he adheres to the concrete stimulus pictures, and the way he develops the characters and plots. Structurally, the patient's responses give information that serves in evaluating mental organization and relationship to reality. The examiner sees the ego's operation in the basic sense of the stories, the relationship of the stories to the stimulus pictures, the adequacy with which the task is carried out, the presence or absence of logical connections among the components of the stories, variations in the use of language, the presence or absence of perceptual or thought distortions, and the appropriateness and quality of integration of affective elements.

Structure and the Clinical Interview

Clinical interviews, like psychological tests, are viewed as conditions that elicit samples of behavior. The interview does not contain a check list of questions to be answered or other specific material that must be covered with each client. The direction the interview will take depends primarily upon the interviewer and his reaction to the person to whom he is relating. Each interviewer has a purpose in mind as well as a theoretical orientation that guides his behavior during the process of the interview. Broadly stated, in the structural framework the purpose is to determine how the client deals with another person. For example, disregarding the meaning of the language used, does the interviewer feel the patient is reaching out toward an object relationship via efforts to find affection; does he feel there is an attempt to control him; does he feel a vague distance or barrier established by the patient; or is the interview simply a mechanical exchange of words? All of these and many additional possibilities are obtained through a running account of the interviewer's as well as the patient's thoughts and feelings as they occur in the interaction process. This does not mean that such data cannot be obtained by the sensitive clinician during testing; it does mean that the psychologist can be more open or relatively free to permit such experiences during the interview.

In the interaction process the interviewer has the chance to shift his stance and experiment with the patient's ability to relate on different footings. Thus, the psychologist is part of the stimulus situation here just as he is during testing. The theoretical orientation is simply that in this more open-ended interpersonal situation, additional demands for object relationships and communications can occur that are valuable in assessment. It is neither possible nor desirable to plan in advance what questions or comments will be presented to the interviewee and so the clinical interview becomes a "thinking on one's feet" arrangement for the individual conducting this process. The interviewer attempts to utilize himself as a "clinical instrument" in that he needs to be able to conceptualize how he experienced the relationship with the patient. This insight into his own reactions becomes important data in the evaluation process.

In discussing the dimensions of goal ambiguity-clarity and stimulus ambiguity-clarity, we stated that interviews can be structured in such a way as to fall into any of the four quadrants of Figure 1 and thus place different demands upon the patient. For example, specific questions asking for specific answers, such as queries regarding the patient's current work or marital status, dates or points in the patient's history, descriptions of experiences in certain situations, information about certain duties, symptoms and behavior in given situations, etc., would fall in quadrant I. Quadrant II-type questions might ask for an elucidation and elaboration of general areas in the patient's life, e.g., work, marriage, sexual relationships, and the like. Here the interviewer would observe how the patient with a given goal relates various elements and brings them to bear on the task along with whether the patient can maintain goal-directed thinking and a circumscribed area of thought. An example of this type of question would be, "Would you tell me about your relationship with your mother?" Quadrant IV questions tax the patient's capacity to synthesize data: the interviewer might present certain aspects of the history, the patient's feelings, and other relevant data contiguously and ask the patient to consider relationships, discover common themes, or relate elements of common concern to one another. Quadrant III has been characterized in terms of leaving the patient relatively more on his own. Thus, the interviewer who gives least directionality and responds minimally can observe the patient's capacity for maintaining a continuous, self-directed, and organized stream of communication.

The interviewer in each context should be alert to the "structural style" of the patient, i.e., the kind of structure or control imposed by the patient on the interview and the interviewer. For example, does he attempt to control the situation by directly or subtly attempting to steer the direction of discussion; does he respond completely within the "givens" of the interviewer and never go beyond, etc.? The discussion does not have to center on dynamic content for such observation, but dynamic qualities may emerge in the role relationships attempted by the patient (e.g., seductive, counter-dependent, etc.).

The basic difference between psychological tests and clinical interviews lies in the degree of standardization. In psychological tests the same stimulus material is presented to the individual in the same order with a rigorous set of administering instructions, although there are, of course, individual differences from tester to tester in subtleties of style of presentation of this material and in subtle and frequently unconscious roles taken. A clinical interview is much less of a standard procedure. The clinical interviewer may present any stimulus he feels is appropriate. However, the stimuli presented are far from random in that interviewers do develop a set of internal norms that they continue to utilize from interview to interview. Thus, we are dealing with a continuum of standardization with psychological tests more standardized than clinical interviews, but with neither totally standardized nor completely lacking in standardization. Needless to say, the examiner's awareness of his own interpersonal predispositions, or his "stimulus value," is of critical importance.

THE INFERENCE PROCESS

Interrelationships of data from various tests

Since the nature of psychological tests is to tax different qualities of ego functioning by virtue of the varying demands the tests present to the ego, it is to be expected that more pathological responses would be more probable in tests that are less directional and/or have greater stimulus ambiguity. Thus, differential weighting is given to inappropriate responses depending upon the particular task from which they derive. As an example of this point, one might consider the following response. To the instruction to define words on the Wechsler-Bellevue (Form I) Vocabulary subtest, the subject responds to the word "shilling" by saying

"England." To an area on Card IX of the Rorschach, another subject says "Russia." The Wechsler-Bellevue response reflects an association to the word "shilling" rather than a definition, thus violating the basic instructions, which are to tell the examiner what the word means. When the subject was questioned about his response, he indicated that he knew a shilling was a coin and he thought it was an English coin. He expected the examiner to understand his unverbalized association when he produced the response, "England." In the Rorschach the other subject was following the instructions to tell what he saw because that portion of Card IX, even though it is an F-, looked like a picture of Russia that he remembered from a map.

Both of these responses reflect something amiss within these two people, but the seriousness is greater in the Wechsler-Bellevue response of the first subject. The reason the Wechsler-Bellevue illustration reflects a greater ego defect is that the subject failed to recognize reality demands when those demands were spelled out clearly via the structure of the test. Also, this defect is more serious because the intelligence test questions do not usually challenge the organizational quality of the ego as much as less structured tests do. Roy Schafer's remark that a little bit of pathology on the Wechsler-Bellevue is worth more than a good bit of pathology on the Rorschach highlights this idea.[3] Even though it is extremely difficult to specify precisely the difference in weighting, it is important to remember that such a differential exists.

These generalizations concerning structure appear to hold true for the majority of individuals who are evaluated. Rather than the consensual reality determinant of structuredness, an individual may react to the tests in terms of the composition or organization of his own ego. A person may be so constricted in his functioning that he is only able to respond to the most concrete components

---

[3] From a lecture at the Menninger Foundation, Topeka, Kansas, October, 1958.

of ambiguous stimuli. Such a person may be able to see only colors, shading, or "inkblots" as responses to the Rorschach. In contrast, another individual may be so disorganized that he is unable to give an "appropriate" response to answer a direct, straightforward question on the Wechsler. Such a person might well begin to associate to a vocabulary item of this test and end up with a chaotic stream of associations. This implies that the examiner must hold the general rules of intrinsic test structure in mind but maintain an alertness to behavioral differences on the part of the subject. In fact, this distortion of test structure by the exceptional patient, rather than being a liability in the assessment process, may serve as a valuable clue to the person's ego organization.

Because the psychologist uses standardized procedures (tests) in his psychological examination, he can be much more analytic of the nature of the demands that he presents to the examinee and of the nature of the reactions that his examination incurs. In less formal styles of examination such as interviewing, the examiner may become more involved in the content elements that form the natural media of intercourse between patient and examiner.

Patients do not always respond as though they recognize the tests as presenting the requirements that the psychologist has defined by implication. The "demand" to tell a story to a TAT picture sometimes produces only descriptive data. Rorschach "percepts" may involve blot descriptions or they may involve the development of a thematic production. Sorting Test groupings may be organized and defined via properties that are symbolic or via a thematic linkage. Such violations, again, offer a view of the quality of ego functioning. The patient's responses form a patterning of his mode of dealing with environmental demands. In their extreme form, such "violations" give clear-cut evidence of gross ego impairment in the capacity to appraise reality and function in linkage with reality. In their subtler forms, such patternings describe a mode of functioning that may bring into perspective styles of ego defect.

The question is often asked why such violations or deviations from the demands of the test situation are considered pathological and cannot be considered creative in a positive sense. As previously mentioned, our definition of creativity includes a reality-syntonic element: the creative individual is free to manipulate ideas, feelings, associations, and objects as much as he can or wishes — but within a reality framework. Or, as Rapaport (1951) defined the creative process: irrational, primitive, fragmented, or primary process thinking is subsequently integrated and elaborated in the framework of logically communicable (secondary) thought processes. The autonomously creative individual regulates his behavior in terms of the demands of the task, although he may devise a variety of ingenious ways of reaching the goal. Even when spontaneous, his behavior shows organization and integration.

Conceptualization of the inference process

The psychologist translates his data and observations into clinically useful information on the basis of his understanding of what functions are sampled and how these functions relate to personality organization. He assumes that his data are the end products of a complex system of functioning and that the behavior being sampled represents the patient's efforts to function adaptively. In other words, the psychological examination is conceived as a segment of the patient's life in which the style and adequacy of his functioning are under scrutiny. The examiner, the testing context, and the tests form a segment of reality against which the patient reacts to yield a sample of his functioning.

The inference process

A central theme of the structural approach is that test data are expressions of the person in the context of demands or requirements to adapt to reality. As such, test data are behavior samples of the adaptive functions of the personality. Viewed in this manner, the meaningfulness of test data can be sought through a "reconstitution" of the system, structure, or patterned hierarchy of adaptive functions through which this behavior was mediated. The term "mediating" is most meaningful in this context. It may be that among methods of test interpretation the "configurational" approach is understood to be the sophisticated approach while data used in a directly interpretive isomorphic manner are scorned. However, the term "configurational" generally means that the data are scrutinized to find a pattern of "best fit" somewhat akin to the concept of rotating factors in factor analysis until there is maximum usage of data and minimum residual. The use of the term "mediating process" in the structural approach supplements the configurational concept by postulating that the test data become meaningful as they point toward an understanding of the ego functions of which they are expressions and the hierarchical organization of such expressions. The entire structure of the ego "mediates" the expression of examination behavior. The clinician goes through a number of steps, implicitly or explicitly, by which he reconstructs a model of his conceptual approximation of the hierarchical ego structure. It is this "model" which constitutes the mediating construct that forms a bridge between test data and extrapolations to other areas of behavior and predictions of the future of the personality.

The interpretive schema in the structural approach does not yield to a test-oriented theory of personality. We do not speak of a "high M" person or someone with a "Dd approach." Neither are data used primarily in a sign approach. That is, an empirical derivation of coded score configurations significantly correlated to various behavior criteria is not seen as a potent mode of utilizing test data in the case of efforts to understand a given patient. Similarly, symbolism which can generally be interpreted via psychoanalytic constructs as revealing specific areas of dynamic

TABLE 1

STEPS IN THE INFERENCE PROCESS*

(1)	(2)	(3)
Test responses, observed behavior, affective reactions, coded scores, clinician's personal reactions.	Symbolic content; relationships of responses to stimuli; coherence and organization of responses; reaction to changes in stimuli; complexity of responses.	Differential patterns of functioning; range of reactions; drive level or intensity; indications of delay or control capacity.
(4)	**(5)**	**(6)**
Relationship of content and structure; cognitive or perceptual patterns; energy deployment; coordination of processes; degree of ego stability.	Formulation of personality dynamics; personality structure; and current level of functioning	Capacity for relationships; capacity for change; points of amenability to change.
	(7)	
	Anticipated course of behavior as extrapolated from above.	

*Derived from Hirt & Kaplan (1967).

conflict are not considered as the means of arriving at a critical understanding of the personality.

Hirt and Kaplan (1967) have conceptualized the inference process in the structural approach as a series of successive steps inductively integrating test data into a patterning that yields to personality constructs: inferences are generated from the data; points of correspondence indicate test patterning; test patterning reflect patterns of ego functioning; higher order constructs are employed to encompass the convergences and lead to a "model" of the ego structure. Once the "model" is constructed, inferences can be drawn deductively as probability statements describing how the personality functions independent of test references or test constructs.

This system of describing the inference process is outlined in Table 1. The sequence of steps starts with column 1, which lists the anchoring data: raw test responses, coded scores and tabulations, observations of the patient's behavior, and the data of the examiner's personal reaction. The first level of inference formation is presented as step 2 (column 2). This step encompasses the clinician's recognition of where the data come from. That is, he begins to order the information about the kind of responses elicited by different stimuli or tasks. He recognizes behavior-context interactions noting the fluctuations in functioning that emerge under different conditions. He is also aware of the context of responses, their complexity, their symbolic significance, their organization, coherence, intellectual level and lapses, or what appear to be confusions or losses of reality contact. This step is really one of scrutinizing and recognizing how behavior emerged in response to the tasks.

In step 3, this system considers the psychologist to be conceptualizing emerging patternings in the test data. He observes the points of overlap or divergence in test constructs. For example, can patterns of weaknesses in functioning be detected in terms of reactions to complexity? ambiguity of test structure? ambiguity of test stimuli? dynamic significance of stimuli? Is there a repetition of patterns of loosening of association and efforts to restrict and control the expression of ideation at these moments? From this overall perspective of test functioning, does the patient appear to have met the implicit test conditions or violated some of the "intrinsic" demands? It is at this point that the matrix model of functions tapped by various tests begins to show utility. The analysis of how the patient is dealing with the tests yields inferences about ego functioning. One gleans information about favored coping strategies, cognitive or perceptual styles, control and range of energy deployment, tolerance for anxiety, ability to control or delay reactions, relationship of content to mode of expression.

In step 5, the psychologist turns more fully to the concept of ego functions that he has been working out and fits them into relationships that are emancipated from their derivation on the tests. The patterning that emerges here is that of ego structure. This is the central step in the inference process. The mediating formulation or "model" is established which represents the examiner's approximation of how the ego constructs form a pattern that corresponds to the patient's behavior pattern. Dynamic concepts are given meaning in relationship to the structural configuration. The patient's current level of functioning is clarified and other sources of data are checked to determine if they are theoretically consistent with the emerging formulation. The formulation also provides a means of scanning back over the earlier inferential steps to locate inconsistencies or gaps that the overall formulation could now encompass or that, perhaps, will not yield to integration and which force the overall formulation to be modified or reconsidered.

Some of the major extrapolations are gained inductively in step 6. The psychologist considers the resources that the person has for carrying on his life, the kinds of relationships of which he is capable, and his experience of his life and of specific events. The overall structure yields an understanding of the stability, vulnerability, or malleability of ego organization and, in step 7, these concepts are applied to whatever requirements apply in the specific case: recommendation for protecting the patient from stress, prescription for technique of strengthening ego functions, the effects of the patient's home life, the function of his work situation in maintaining or weakening his organization.

Needless to say, these steps are an effort at an approximation of the inference process rather than a description of the steps through which a clinician mechanically proceeds. In the chapters that follow, the cases are presented in a manner that attempts to reproduce the steps taken by the clinicians in reaching the mediating formulations of ego structure and the derivative understandings of how the patients experience themselves and their world, and what steps are needed to develop appropriate therapeutic strategies.

CHAPTER IV

Schizophrenia: Faulty Ego Synthesis

STRUCTURAL FORMULATION OF SCHIZOPHRENIA

From a structural point of view, schizophrenia is a phenomenon of ego defect. The pathology is seen as a psychological problem of perhaps varying etiology but representing an impairment in the basic mechanisms of personality that maintain internal organization and contact with reality. Structural theory describes the nature of the defect and facilitates an understanding of what happens to the organism under different conditions of functioning. Three basic assumptions of the structural approach in schizophrenia can be delineated as follows:

(1) Schizophrenia is an impairment in the hierarchical organization of the ego. This impairment leaves three basic processes vulnerable to disorganization. The three processes can be separated conceptually in terms of function but their functioning is highly interactional. The processes are: internal organization, synchrony of adaptive processes with the environment, and coordination and continuity of experience over time.

(2) While the impairment in ego organization is recognized as basic to schizophrenia, there are shifts between different phases of the schizophrenic condition. These changes are assumed to reflect disruptions in equilibrium between ego impairment and ego adaptive functioning (as from latent to acute conditions) or to reflect the regaining of equilibrium (as from acute to remission).

(3) The structural approach recognizes variability of functioning within any given phase. Confusion or disorganization difficulties encountered in any of the ego functions strain the

hierarchical organization and raise danger of precipitous general disorganization. On the other hand, clarity and sharpness of reality testing prompt organized functioning which fosters better organization and this organization, in turn, facilitates coordination in other portions of the hierarchical system.

It is important to stress that the system being described is one of interactive psychological processes that maintain effective existence as long as they function. When the conditions necessary for its existence are absent, ego functioning breaks down or ceases to exist as psychological structure. These necessary conditions involve the synchronization of ego processes with reality and the inner organization of processes in a coherent, integrated functional unity. The point of entry or the point of initiation of disorganization appears most critically at the point of loss of contact or loss of discrimination between "inner" and "outer," or in Federn's terms, "cathexes" are withdrawn from the bodily boundaries. This is a phenomenon that leaves the schizophrenic individual psychologically undifferentiated and boundless and the ego as a complex organization ceases to function (and to exist). Under these circumstances, the schizophrenic no longer has the means to experience himself as a stable and reliable subject of his own experiences. He has not lost his needs, urges, or strivings; he has lost the means of organized experience, organized expression, and the means of adaptation. He has lost his sense of experience as a finite person in time and space.

In this description of the schizophrenic condition we lean heavily on the theoretical description given by DesLauriers (1962). Under conditions of loss of ego organization or ego integrity, most of the schizophrenic's ego functions (or part processes) are left intact, but they do not operate as functions of an integrated ego; their effectiveness in adaptation is relatively useless and, to the observer, the schizophrenic's efforts appear bizarre, meaningless, inappropriate, and autistic. The ego functions that involve perception, concept formation, thinking, feeling, emotional expression, and motor behavior are not destroyed. But their operations are not brought into synchronization and do not contribute to the individual's existence as a unitary person because they have no unified anchorage or internal organization and cannot yield the experience of a unitary being. The schizophrenic may be driven; he may act, feel, think, and struggle to seek meaning and gratification. There is yearning for coherence and meaningful experience which can be realized only through contact with reality. The schizophrenic's behavior may be disorganized but forced; arbitrary constructions can be understood as desperate efforts to create order to bind feelings and thoughts and to give them some organization, and thus evoke some sense of oneself as a being.

In acute schizophrenia the ego undergoes the kind of disorganization described above. However, when the schizophrenic individual is not in an acute state of disorganization, he nevertheless still suffers from a basic condition of faulty ego synthesis. He has not built up within himself the synthetic function (or the intact hierarchical system of organization) and basic ego integration that firmly interlocks with reality. He has, instead, some form of substitute or compensatory system. It is this form of organization that we observe in "disguised" cases of schizophrenia (latent, ambulatory, incipient, pseudo-neurotic), or in schizophrenia in remission. The problem of the non-acute schizophrenic is that of maintaining his organization, avoiding loss of contact with reality, and avoiding ego disorganization. In our clinical histories of schizophrenic patients or in our psychological examinations of non-acute schizophrenics, we are able to detect behavior which fits a conception of this chronic struggle to escape psychosis. There is, typically, evidence of continuous efforts to concretize a sense of identity and concurrently there is a chronic inability to free oneself from this struggle. The patterns vary but they can be understood as having a common theme: the basic lack of ego synthesis. One person may have lived a barren existence in which he has apparently developed few or no object relations, living in a concrete world of routine tasks and drifting aimlessly. Another may show much more affect and evidence of apparent neurotic developments, but also reveal a subtle pattern of functioning in a circumscribed existence within an environmental structure from which deviation cannot be tolerated.

In conditions of acute schizophrenia and rapid recovery the symptoms are sharp and clear, but as the problems of latent conditions or problems of borderline chronicity are encountered, this clarity fades out. This lack of clear understanding is mainly due to the absence of a conceptual system that would help us understand the interrelationship of the various behavior manifestations or symptoms. The concept of faulty ego synthesis offers the possibility of leading toward an understanding of the relationship between defect and adaptive effort. Some of the schizophrenic person's behavior is a result of inadequacy or defect; some of his behavior is compensatory or an effort at adaptation and stability.

The relationship of adaptive effort to ego defect may be brought into perspective with an analogy. Consider the possibility of several earthmen landing separately on other planets and discovering life there. In each case the earthman has no way to return home. He finds the inhabitants and cultural setting of life on this foreign planet extremely strange. He must remain where he is, presumably for life, and he finds the task of adjustment extremely difficult. The inhabitants communicate in a way that has impact on him, but with a disconcerting lack of familiarity or comprehensibility.

In this situation our earthmen must attempt to adapt with whatever knowledge and personality resources they have. In the context of this profoundly confusing situation, one of our spacemen might attempt an adaptation by restricting his mode of operations to very narrow and manageable segments of time and space. He could restrict his areas of effort and passively await the next demand upon him without extending himself into unknown dangers. To a large degree he would be helpless in attempting to gain perspective on his total situation, but he might be able to exist within his narrow framework.

The second earthman might feel hopelessly confused by the strange stimuli that are so out of his ken. His pattern of response might be chaotic effort in all directions at once with resultant maladaptive behavior, although out of this welter of confusion an occasional appropriate response hits the mark almost by accident. This man would not only feel intense discomfort but also feel unable to gain direction or to organize his efforts, and his behavior would constantly endanger him.

Our third earthman attempts to learn some cues or manifestations that he could fit into a pattern. He does not really know or understand what he is dealing with, but he tries to find consistencies or discriminations that seem to work and he weaves them together in terms of hypotheses that derive from earth experience. As long as they work he feels reassured; when they fail he feels lost, unable to regain his bearings, and he makes desperate efforts to force his experience into possible systems.

Each of these three people so transplanted attempts a mode or pattern of coming to grips or finding stability in the strange new environment, a pattern that draws on his inner resources. The pattern is comprehensible in terms of efforts to adapt to an environment with which one has had no experience and which fails to fall into stable discernible discriminations or patterns of organization. The conditions that have been described are fanciful circumstances. However, our comparison is to earthmen on earth where the problem of schizophrenia is conceived as being within the person rather than as a product of environmental conditions. The problem of adaptation to reality in the context of personalities lacking ego synthesis is akin to that of the struggle with environments that have varying degrees of strangeness or incomprehensibility. The person engaged in the struggle experiences the world around him in a manner which we theorize as analogous to a normal person in an environment with some degree of strangeness.

The case illustrations to follow are presented as real life counterparts to the paradigm of earthmen coping with alien worlds. The cases were selected because they present illuminating contrasts into the variety of conditions that may develop in the absence of the synthetic function. In each of the cases, the focal points of discussion will be the manner in which inner ego processes are organized, the manner in which the organism relates to reality, the manner in which the personality structure finds or struggles for some locus of organization, and the manner in which he presumably "experiences." It will be one of the tasks of our discussion to understand each unique pattern of defect in combination with the particular pattern of adaptation as it exists in the individual under examination.

CHAPTER V

Mr. B: Mechanical Man

On guard duty one night, a 21-year-old serviceman shot and killed his partner on duty. There had apparently been no quarrel or argument. The serviceman could offer no explanation. His past service record had been uneventful. The preparation for court martial included psychiatric and psychological examination. The serviceman was described as affectless, uninvolved and suggestible, yet organized. There was no evidence of primary process functioning with delusions, hallucinations, or fusions. In fact, the various ego functions showed some stability. The formulation of his personality and the hypothesized explanation offered for his behavior rested on the diagnosis of a faulty ego synthesis, and what follows is an analysis of the test materials used in reaching this conclusion. The test protocols are reproduced beginning on page 93.

The main features of behavior
in relation to structural concepts

There are several characteristic features of personality that can be described to gain a perspective of this person. The style of functioning is remarkable in its sterile quality which, although subtle at many points, is so pervasive that it forms a strikingly clear picture of a certain form of ego defect. The patient's style is that of a segmental process; the patient's behavior appears to be made up of sequences comprehensible as responses to discrete stimuli. Each segment utilizes various part or fragmentary ego processes so that memory, thought, perception, cognition, affect, etc. are evident and maintain themselves as discrete functions. The element of gross deficiency is precisely that of overall unity and continuity over time. This aspect is apparent in two ways: (1) in the patient's manner of behaving he relates to fractional elements rather than to wider aspects of what might be considered the wholeness of reality demands placed on him; (2) we fail to discern qualities of the use of self or individuality as an ingredient or baseline for experience. In both of these ways it appears that responses are being made to stimuli, but the total organism is not quite "with it" as a participant. The inference is that it is a lack of organism as participant that creates the absence of meaningful incorporation of any given behavior segment into the ongoing stream of behavior — such incorporation being necessary for the continuity of the organism as a psychological entity. In the following paragraphs we shall discuss specific features of the patient's record revealing these characteristic aspects.

The patient's productions show a "pattern of mechanical reacting." The quality of direct, unreflective responsiveness is a sharp feature of the record. The patient frequently appears to react "off the top of his head," or to react with a variety of possibilities but without noticeable effort to screen or evaluate or to impose judgment as to what is more or less relevant or important among the possibilities entertained. We do not observe reactions as to the correctness of responses, or subsequent efforts on the examinee's part to modify, enhance, alter, or embellish what he has given. This gives rise to the suspicion that he is not engaging in a self-conscious screening or self-evaluating process. At other points the patient appears to respond without an apparent system. In the BRL Sorting Test, objects are reacted to and associations are formed in piecemeal sequence without evidence of the development of an overall pattern for each grouping. One idea appears to prompt the next as though the whole is a chain of connections rather than one with overall continuity. In this serial pattern, various conceptual categories are encountered or triggered by concrete, immediate relationships, but these are lost as new categories and new associations emerge. The patient exhausts the conceptual possibilities without selectivity. For example, he responds to the red rubber ball by first adding the red paper disk for reason of "redness" and then the cigar, sink stopper, and eraser because they are all rubber like the ball. However, it occurs to him at this point that one plays with a ball; so a number of presumed "play" items are thrown in. And so he continues to add items by reason of concrete identity, metallic composition, texture, smoking function, paper composition, and, finally, the syncretistic rationalization that they are all "essential in some way."

The serial flow observed in the first BRL response has its counterpart in the flow of ideas occasionally observed in the Rorschach. This flow is accompanied by phenomena of apparent lack of discrimination or judgment between clear, easily integrated responses and those that lack such qualities. The response to Card II which indicates that the patient sees the face of an animal and the body of a human is an example of the serial process where there are immediate, narrow, poorly integrated perceptual acts. One part is tacked onto another part rather than yielding to a broader integration that would bring the parts into consonance with reality.

A similar pattern is observed in the TAT responses. Events happen to people without consideration for antecedent causes, nor is there adherence to the postulate that since the characters are constant, the theme must develop an integrated relationship around the people involved. Instead, the TAT picture is used as a stimulus, a starting point, with a chain-like serial production in which an idea is triggered by its immediate predecessor but with no overall unification or referral to earlier elements.

The significance of this behavior in structural terms lies in its indication of a lack of those internal processes that function to organize: formulating a contextual pattern, selectively screening, integrating, or eliminating in terms of judgments of relevancy to overall themes. We can think of the patient as operating as though he were stimulus bound rather than goal directed. This term refers to the idea that a person is guided by external stimuli that intrude on the sensory apparatus rather than being guided by ongoing internal systems.

Another feature of this record is that the patient produces *units of behavior that appear to be narrow and stereotyped.* The observation has been made that the patient's thought processes operate predominantly in a narrowly focused form rather than directed by broader perspectives. However, the contents of the narrow focus have some special features. The patient typically offers a series of cliché-like or stereotyped units. What is included in the series seldom shows originality and it seldom shows very specific relevance to the immediate situation at hand. The impression is that of a stock of standard or overlearned units that are related by a form of learned pathways or associations, but with little in the way of higher ego functions that select, relate, and control associations and give meaning in terms of what the person wishes to communicate. This makes the stilted style of the TAT stories more comprehensible. Frequently the serial constructions present no integrated theme and it is apparent that the patient was without goal or direction as he produced the story. This is manifest in such an illogical construction as his story of a woman who caused her husband's death but then "lived happily ever after." What is produced at a given moment fits the requirements of that moment if we consider a narrow segment of attention in time and space. The appropriate unit of interaction — the total story that this man must produce to the card, or a relationship to the examiner, or his behavior in the total setting — is not readily apparent.

Together with the manner in which this person responds and the quality of that which he produces, our concern is also directed to the characteristics to which the patient directs his attention. The content of what the patient attends to can frequently be described as something less than the totality of the situation that is imposed upon him. Just as the unit of behavior has been described as narrow, so the *unit of attention focus* frequently is only a segment or sub-segment of the stimulus imposed upon the patient. To describe a Rorschach concept as having "a body of a human and face of an animal" may be labeled an arbitrary integration, but it indicates that at a basic level the patient begins with and sticks to perceptual organizational units that are merely parts of or less than whole considerations of units in reality. His ability to create integrated and meaningful perceptual relationships is defective.

We are led to the hypothesis that this person's ego structure can most easily cope with situations which represent sharp, narrow, discrete kinds of environmental demand situations. The test records are impressive in the clarity of an overall *pattern of differential functioning between situations of clear, definitive conditions and those of more ambiguous, open-end test conditions.* This pattern is illustrated by the BRL Test where this man responds to the pre-selected sortings (passive portion of this test) as though their conceptualizations were simple, obvious tasks, and his responses are comparatively adequate. In the active portion of the test where he must conceptually organize the test material, his functioning is much more awkward. Similarly, the Wechsler imposes demands which are fairly clear in what they require of the patient, and his functioning on this test is relatively adequate. In those portions of the Rorschach where the blot characteristics have more "card pull," more adequate responses are elicited than in those areas where there is more ambiguity and complexity.

The differential pattern indicates that under one set of conditions — clarity of behavioral cues — the patient can function in greater harmony and in greater consonance with reality. In support of this idea is the observation that the patient appears to make efforts to elicit clarity, or cues, or signals that would serve the purpose of prompting appropriate behavior in him. His behavior in the test situation was marked by a quality of passive waiting for signals and for reactions to his expressions to help him determine direction and further response.

THE ABSENCE OF THE SYNTHETIC FUNCTION

When we bring together the various patterns that have been noted, those of automatic or mechanical reacting, cue seeking, familiar or stereotyped segments of behavior, and responsiveness to discrete stimuli, we note that they form a complex of functioning that is distinctive and comprehensible with the structural framework. This complex is seen as distinctive in its deficit of just those characteristics that define the synthetic function of the ego: integration, coordination, functioning as a totality, and experience as an integral unit of interaction with external reality. This, of course, has been implied at many points in the discussion where the element under observation indicated something less than adequate ability to discern or react to the relatedness or unity of experience.

Since, in this case, the most notable deficit is the lack of those processes which organize and interrelate various sub-processes, we also assume that the experience of unity which depends on these processes cannot be maintained. The experience of being a continuous organism in an organized state co-exists with the organism's utilization of ego processes that guide, direct, screen, and check the ongoing stream of mental activity. These processes not only serve the function of maintaining goal-directed adaptive behavior but also create the means by which the organism gains an overview and experiences himself as an ongoing entity. If the processes that give integration and coordination to mental events do not function, the person no longer has the ability to experience cause and effect, or to localize sources of experience, or to anticipate effects of behavior. He not only loses a systematic inner awareness of what occurs within him, but he also loses the sense of meaningful participator or interactor with the environment. This has profound implications. Things happen not to the self but in a panorama of groundless experience. Ideas come, not in interrelationship, one prompting the other, but in a form of hectic "free association" of external stimuli and internal reactions to these stimuli.

The implications regarding what this man experiences are very strongly in the direction that his existence is, in many respects, meaningless to him. Without a synthetic function creating unitary participation in interaction with the environment, it is difficult for him to generate a set of ongoing goals, wishes or strivings. It is difficult to experience a sense of awareness of self in relationship to one's productions or of self in relationship to the future of the self. The implications of this phenomenon are apparent in the patient's behavior. There is a gross lack of what might be called personal or emotional involvement. What he produces has a flat, empty quality. Little in the test material or test situation appears more or less important, more or less strange, more or less common, more or less relevant. There is little that appears related to this man's life, his values, or his desires.

Adaptation without synthetic function

The pattern described in this patient contains "elements of functioning stability" as well as ego deficit. Perhaps the concern in evaluating this person as having a defective ego, as we have done, rests on the expectation that such a state of affairs must be accompanied by an evidence of a breakdown of structure with primary process expression in delusions, hallucinations, diffusions, etc. However, in this man, functioning is not totally absent or collapsed. Strangely, part processes appear to operate with some stability. This person perceives, recalls, recognizes, and has some self-evaluative capacity so that his behavior is generally confined within society's limits of acceptance. It is, in fact, the capacity for part process functioning to proceed that provides the explanation for some maintenance of stability and organization. His function-ing can be conceptualized from two perspectives: he *lacks* the ego functions that emerge out of a synthesis of self-experience so that his functioning is deficient in interrelationship of person to reality;

he *has* part process "ego" functions that can serve a system of piecemeal adaptation of moment-to-moment contact with concrete environmental segments. Heavy reliance on a cue-directed, narrow, unreflective mode of operating appears pathological in one sense but it also reduces demands on the defective integratirg and coordinating functions. This is a mode of existence and it "succeeds" as long as it serves the patient in avoiding confusion and disorganization. This pattern is somewhat similar conceptually to the constricted and concretistic pattern frequently observed as a defensive adaptation in brain damaged individuals. Our man functions within the limits of a personality that is not able to develop a global focus. The segmental units that are observed serve at least to keep psychological phenomena within the bounds of order when the environment provides enough stimuli or data to support his mechanical efforts.

TEST PROTOCOLS OF MR. B

Wechsler-Bellevue I

	R.S.	Wt. S		
Inf.	14	10		
Com.	11-12	10-11		
Dig.	14	13		
Arith.	6-7	7-9		
Sim.	12	10		
Verb.		50-3	Verbal IQ	104-108
P.A.	15	13	Perf. IQ	104
P.C.	12	12	Full Sc. IQ	105-107
Blks.	24	11		
Dig. S.	30	7		
Perf.		54		
Total		104-7		

Information

1.	Before — Dwight D. Eisenhower; Truman.	1
2.	Therm — Measures degrees - heat.	1
3.	Rubber — Trees.	1

4.	London – England.	1
5.	Pints – 2.	1
6.	Weeks – 52.	1
7.	Italy – Spain – Madrid – wait a minute, can't think of it.	0
8.	Heart – Pumps blood.	1
9.	Brazil – South America.	1
10.	Japan – Tokyo.	1
11.	Plane – Wright Brothers.	1
12.	Tall – 5 ft. 4 in., I guess.	1
13.	Paris – I think 4000.	0
14.	Hamlt – Shakespeare.	1
15.	Popn – 170 million.	1
16.	Wash – Feb. 12, I think.	0
17.	Pole – Byrd or Dewey – not sure.	0
18.	Egyp – Europe.	0
19.	Finn – Mark Twain.	1
20.	Vati – Not sure – a book.	0
21.	Kora – Don't know.	0
22.	Faust – O'Henry? Not sure.	0
23.	Corp – Can't think of that.	0
24.	Ethn – Don't know.	0
25.	Apoc – Don't know.	0

Score   14

Comprehension

1.	Env – Put it in a mail box.	2
2.	Thea – Notify someone – manager or someone. If small, get extinguisher and put it out myself, at same time call somebody.	2
3.	B.C. – Bad influence. Might do something bad yourself. Might get you into trouble.	2-1
4.	Tax – Keep the U.S. going (Q) To have freedom – need money.	2
5.	Shoe – Because gives – does not break and is flexible.	1
6.	Land – 'Cause more likely to be used for something to build something better on.	1
7.	For – Sun (Q) Comes out of West and goes to East – just look up and see where it is.	0
8.	Law – To govern the people. Keeps things uniform, (Q) orderly.	1

9.	Mar – So they'll know who is married – eligibility to marry each other.	0
10.	Deaf – Can't hear themself – don't know how sound.	1

Score   11-12

Arithmetic

1.	4 + 5? (1″) 9.	1
2.	6c - 10? (1″) 4.	1
3.	8c - 25? (1″) 17.	1
4.	or 36, or 4? (3″) 9.	1
5.	2 hrs 24 mi, 3 mph? (1″) 8.	1
6.	7 2c-50? (21″) 36.	1
7.	7 lb 25, $1? (65″) Simple, but can't think 28.	0-1
8.	2/3 new, 400? (45″) 275, no 1200, no 800.	0
9.	5? (45″).	0
10.	1 man? (25″).	0

Score   6-7

Similarities

1.	Or-Ba	– Fruits.	2
2.	Ct-Dr	– Clothes, dress up in them.	2
3.	Dg-Ln	– Animals.	2
4.	Wn-Bi	– Means of transportation.	2
5.	Pa-Ra	– Means of information.	2
6.	Ar-Wr	– Both have to do with outdoors.	0
7.	Wo-Al	– Alcohol comes from wood.	0
8.	Ey-Er	– Both needed by a person to get along.	0
9.	Eg-Sd	– Egg can produce a chicken; seed can produce something useful.	0
10.	Po-St	– On base of some statues have poems; only thing I can think of.	0
11.	Pr-Pu	– Both can affect a person in a certain way.	1
12.	Fl-Tr	– Both need air.	1

Score   12

Picture Completion

1.	Gl	1	9.	Wch	1
2.	Mn	1	10.	Pchr	1

3.	Mn – no ears and also he's wearing lipstick	1	11.	Mr		1
			12.	Mn – Don't have a tie on		1
4.	Cd	1	13.	Bib		1
5.	Cr – Main part of body	0	14.	GI – Can't see ear		0
6.	Pg	1	15.	Sh – Trees don't grow on deserts		0
7.	Bt	1			Score	12
8.	Dr	1				

Digit Span

Digits Forward	8	Digits Backward		6
			Score	14

Picture Arrangement

Hse	3″	PAT	2	
Hold	29″	LMNO	2	Take man in trial holdup – (doesn't see court scene)
Elev	5″	ABCD	2	Okay
Flirt	19″	AJNET	2	Okay
Fish	39″	SAMUEL	4	
Taxi	50″	EFGHIJ	3	Gets heavy so calls taxi...shamed and flushed, so ...

Score 15

Block Design

A.

B.   (Much trouble using all 1/2s)

1.	13	+	4
2.	13	+	4

3.	13	+	4	(Slow and methodological)
4.	34	+	3	
5.	53	+	3	
6.	150	+	3	(One off at 100″) That's right (corrects)
7.	170	+	3	
		Score	24	

BRL Sorting Test

PART I

STIMULUS OBJECT	SORT AND VERBALIZATION	SCORE
Ball (Free Choice)	Nothing goes with it. (Encouraged) Red paper is round like it and it's rubber so this goes. So is this cigar, sink stopper, eraser is rubber and ball you play with, so hammer, saw, pliers, toy cigarette, and dice, sugar. With the hammer, nails go with it and nail related to wood block, screwdriver related to play things and screwdriver related to screwdriver and pliers related to screwdriver. Pliers are metal, so are knife, fork, spoon, bell; knife, fork, spoon go with knife, fork, spoon. Lock metal — corks are texture like ball, cigarette with the cigar. Pipe smokes like cigar, match to light cigar. Cigarette like cigar. Red paper with circle so green and	

	white with paper. ("Why do they belong together?") All–all essential in some way.	Chain L
Pipe	Cigarette, cigar, matches, (pipe is wood), wood block (corn pipe, but looks like wood). Screw-driver is wood. I could put all the stuff with the pipe. Do you want that? (Question) I'll put back all but one cigar, one cigarette, matches. Pipe needs tobacco and can get tobacco from cigarette or cigar. Matches to light it.	C n
Toy Pliers	Saw, hammer. That's all. (Q) They're play toys and come together.	CD n
Fork	Spoon, knife, knife, fork, spoon. (Q) All eating utensils. Use plastic ones for outdoor parties.	CD S/N
Paper Disk	Three papers. (Q) All paper.	CD n
Bell	Nothing belongs with it. (Q) Bell goes on bike and nothing here goes with a bike. Wait – need screwdriver to screw it on.	c

PART II

SORT	VERBALIZATION	SCORE
Smoking	All have something to do with smoking.	CD
Metal	All metal.	CD

Round	All something used daily – all used – all commonly used every day for something.	Syn
Tools	All used for building and fixing different things.	FD
Paper	All paper.	CD
Doubles	Two of every one of them and one is ...	CD
Red	All reddish color.	CD
Silver	Eating utensils.	CD
Rubber	Rubber.	CD
White	White.	CD
Toys	Can all be used as toys.	CD
Rectangles	All come from tree.	Syn

Rorschach Protocol

FREE RESPONDING	INQUIRY
I. 10″ 1. Well it could look like a face. 2. Part of it looks like a bat. 60″ All I can see in it.	1. Of some animal. (Q) Something like a wildcat; no, wolf; eyes slanted, like a wolf but mouth isn't full. (Q) Something between and no forehead. Appears fierce. (Q) Eyes. W, S, F + A (Fab) 2. Wings spread out like flying-claws; head like a bat. (upper 1/2 of W) FM + A P
II. 7″ 1. This one looks like a– two red-headed funny shaped men with their left hand on each other and feet. Dancing or	1. It's a cartoon of a – in funny books – tall head – looks like dancing or fixing to fight. Hands and feet close together. Hands connected; birdlike face. (Q) Not

something. Also looks
like they're boxing.
65" All I can see in it.

men — would have to be funny
looking men. Face like a bird.
Bodies of a bear. Like Woody
Woodpecker or Henry Hawk
cartoon. W M (H)

Also looks like a rocket. (S)
something you see in science fiction movies—front—wide wings &
exhaust. (Right now) taking off—
red is exhaust fumes (Add: S,
D_1, Fm, CF+ Obj.)

III.   14" 1. This looks like two
            people—monkeys or some-
            thing holding something
            in their hands.
        V   2. This way it reminds me
            of some comical face.
        65" That's all.

1. Dark — don't know what's in
hands. (People or monkeys)
Monkeys (Q) The way the heads
are shaped. (Q) Back sticking out
— facing each other. Right arm
missing. W FM + A (P)
2. Ears missing. Could be cartoon
character. Andy Panda. Mouth
and nose missing. This doesn't
look like mouth but in right place.
(Q) Could look like comic character — also looks sadfaced or
something. Could be sad — eyes
droop. D3 F→ M- (H)

IV.   20" 1. This looks like some
            kind of bird — also looks
            like a bug.
            2. Also looks like the —
            under a kangaroo. Look-
            ing at a kangeroo from
            under the bottom — tail —
            big feet —
        70" That's all.

1. Wings or feet. Looks a little
like a turtle too; face of something;
bug. (Q) Wings of bird only (Q)
Turtle legs — this could be turtle
legs too, but facing wrong way —
and if different shaped head —
skull here. W F -A (Contam.)
2. Tall — feet — arms. Except
kangaroo's arms don't stick out
like that. Only chin.
W F-A

V.   2" 1. This looks like a bat.
          2. Or a butterfly.
      45" That's all I see.

1. Antennae (Q) Flying — anything. It's black — the way the
feet come out. W FM, FC + A P

2. Butterfly — reversed — this
antenna — wings — wings — flying
too. W FM+ A P

VI. 20" 1. This reminds me after   1. Hanging on something. (Q)
     V   a kill and you take skin   Outside. Inside would be
           and hang it up — pelt   smoother. This more like hair.
     60"   All I see in this.   (Q) Fuzziness — dull.
                                       W Fc + A Obj. P

VII. 10" 1. Looks like someone —   1. Could be animals more
           fat person — with two   likely — wide head. (Q) Animals
           heads and middle part of   don't have two heads. Siamese —
           body is missing.   connected together; inside miss-
           2. This way looks like a   ing. (Q) Arms; legs.
           cat — with top of fore-   W F - (H)
           head and mouth and nose   2. (Pleasant or unpleasant)
           missing; in other words a   (Q) Odd — not unpleasant.
     75"   cat with no face.   W F- Ad

VIII. 10" 1. This looks like two   1. Tree or branch. (Panthers
           pink panthers or some-   pink?) No, black. Could be
           thing. Climbing up a   another animal. Could be a squir-
           tree. Each coming up on   rel with a tail.
           opposite sides.   DW FM A (P)
           2. This way it looks like   2. Eyes, jaws, mouth, ears are a
           a face with a few parts   little different. (Q) Fierce, I'd
           missing. Face of an ani-   say. (Q) Tigers look fierce.
           mal — to be exact, the   W F → FM- Ad
     90"   face of a tiger. All I see.

IX. 8"   1. All I see in it is the   1. No forehead. No eyes. Bottom
           shape of a wildcat's face. of face is kinda square. No mouth.
                                       Fierce; unpleasant
                                       WF → FM-Ad

X.   15″   1. This looks like the top part of . . . This is two monkeys with a bar between them.

1. Not facing – looks like backs to it – arms reaching up to it. D 3 FM + A

2. Bottom of it looks like a rabbit's face.

2. Ears, nose, eyes. Don't know about this part. D7 F+ Ad P

3. Another part – see two yellow animals – got faces like a dog and bodies like a . . some bodies.

3. Big eyes – not dog's bodies – too small. (Q) Big . . . D10 F A

4. This places looks like a spider – blue splotch.

4. Lots of legs. D1 F+ A P

5. Another thing here – looks like two sea horses.

5. Nose is a little short. Something in back of head shouldn't be here. D9 F+ A

6. Another thing looks like it's jumping from one place to another.

6. Cricket – now frog – no face – can't see face. D6 FM + A

7. Another place looks like a wishbone. All I see

7. The way it comes out. D12 F+ A Obj.

170″   here.

TAT

1. Well, this boy – he has a violin and he's taking lessons but he doesn't like it and now he's supposed to be taking lessons but he's thinking about being outside playing and he keeps playing the violin and his father wants him to be a great violinist and he wants to be something else. His mother wants him to be a violinist most, and after she dies his father isn't so strict on him and tells him to be what he wants to be, and the the boy leaves and comes back a year later and is a great violinist. He couldn't give up the violin – he was used to it – and his father is proud of him.

2. Let's see – This girl just came from school and her father is plowing and her mother just told her to go inside and cook something – do some work, and she doesn't like her mother. Her mother appears to be mean. Afterwhile she – finishes school and she goes off to be an actress and her mother thinks she should

support her. So mother has been working hard and she's a nice girl so figures she should help her mother, so she sends her quite a bit of money. After awhile she has enough money so girl won't send any more so mother gets after and keeps after the girl to send money, so girl finally takes off somewhere and mother never hears from her again.

4. This appears
   This man is — he . . . .
   He's working on a job and his best friend — he was up for a promotion and his friend lies to the foreman and gets the man's job and the man found out when he got home. He's heading out now to fight with this man and his wife tries to stop him. This man was a villain anyway. He finally catches up with him and fights and wins. Makes villain tell truth. Villain gets fired and he gets promotion.

Feel — friend — doesn't understand — then realizes he was acting like a friend to get the promotion. Maybe not a friend after all.

18 GF. This one — This is an old couple living in a house by themselves and this lady's husband was sick and had to go upstairs and she had to go somewhere and leave him in the house by himself. He had some pills he had to have for heart attack or die and the pills were downstairs and he had an attack and tried to get to the pills and fell down and she came back and he almost died. She talked to him for awhile and he died.

She feel? She's broke up because she made mistake of leaving pills downstairs and she feels she killed him and is responsible. (Do?) She has funeral — then couldn't marry again so she moved in with her daughter and lived happily ever after.

18 BM. Here this man is drunk and he is walking down the street going home and passes through a dark alley and someone grabbed

him, but he isn't really drunk — he's a detective and is playing drunk. This is close to a swank night club and people get robbed so they decided to catch the man who does it. The detective knows judo and apprehends the man and takes him in and they question him about all the robberies and find he's been the one and confesses — lock him up — trial — gets two to three years for robbery and assault.

3 BM. Is this a gun down here? Let's see. 30″ This woman when she was a girl she ran away from home and got in with wrong company and started taking dope and stuff and she's been on this stuff three or four years now and hard to get money so she was trying to get money for dope and couldn't. She wanted to so bad she decided to kill herself so she got a gun . . . and shot herself. She first wrote a note why she committed suicide and they found note and told parents who almost had forgotten her — disowned her — they were sad when they heard. After that her parents had some money so they opened a recreation center for teenage boys and girls so that wouldn't happen again and it helped quite a bit.

13 MF. This man he's married and he decided he wants to play a while on his wife, so goes out and gets a woman and has relations with her quite a bit. So after a while she got pregnant and told him if he didn't give her money all the time she'd tell police and his wife. He loved his wife so he was scared and strangled her. Police traced him, asked questions, and found out that he was seen with her last, so police went to his house. He was alone. Took him to headquarters and interrogated him and found he did it. Said no for a while — said he did it and wife was surprised. Said her husband couldn't do it. Had trial and he got life in prison. He paid for his crime. His wife and kids went to see him now and then, and he was good so he got out in 20 years and then everything was okay.

12 M. Well, let's see.

This man was trying to be a hypnotist and make money doing it before an audience, but every time he tried before an audience he couldn't and was ridiculed, and kept trying. He found out he was doing something wrong. He was down to his last penny so finally went for a place to do it, but no one would hire him. Found one guy who said he would have to work for him until he worked it off if he failed. In papers — scared, but tried — before children. They laughed. Another man did it nothing happened to put on great act — fame and thankful.

15. This started in an old English town a long time ago. Man was acting odd, weird, and he was always trying to do something different. Went to graveyard with a man he hired and was trying to build a monster so he could rule the world. So he got body and told his helper to go to brain college and get a brain. Brains were being studied of a mad man and a scholar. The doctor, a weird guy, sent him to get the brain of the scholar. Instead, the helper gets mad brain — transplanted brain. When finished, something went wrong — turned on him and choked him. Then monster got bad and lightening struck him and flood took the whole thing away.

CHAPTER VI

Mrs. K: Kaleidoscopic Experience

A young, stout woman who alternates between silly laughter and childishly seductive verbalizations and gestures is our second case. She is a psychiatric hospital patient who has been severely disturbed for many years. With the obvious bizarreness that she expresses there are variations so that at times she shows a glimmer of insightfulness about her condition accompanied by signs of anxiety and terror. The problem for the examiner was to bring greater understanding to the pattern of her functioning with the goal of devising an effective treatment program. The test protocols are reproduced beginning on page 111.

In the case of Mr. B, the distinction between relatively intact part process organization and relatively absent higher coordination functions appeared helpful in understanding his behavior. In this case the patient's difficulties cut across this distinction. We can, at one moment, observe organized coordination and, in the next, a total lapse of part processes as well as of overall coordination. At times behavior appears to lose all semblance of organization, and this woman flounders helplessly in a "kaleidoscope" of experience in which she loses her sense of identity and of existence.

THE QUALITY OF DISORGANIZATION

The described lapses might be conceptualized as outpourings of primitive material subsequent to defense breakdown. However, the lapses have more specific characteristics which help delineate such events as stemming from a structural problem with particular attributes. The lapses occur under given conditions. They are characterized by disorganization that appears progressively and simultaneously in three phases: loss of coordination with reality, breakdown in systematic relationship among ego part processes (with resultant confusion among affects, thoughts and motor behavior), and loss of locus of identity. These features, of course, are all characteristic and distinctive of absence of synthetic function. The observed alternation in functioning raises the question of whether synthetic function exists when functioning appears more adequate and fades away when ego functioning lapses. We can answer this question if we analyze more closely the manner in which this patient functions. Examination of test behavior indicates that, in a given sequence, stimuli initially elicit relevant trains of thought and also appear to tap intact areas of conceptual capacity. With this kind of beginning, the patient frequently is able to hold to a course which produces material that tells us that, while an appropriate area of conceptualization had been initially prompted, the response that developed was not a properly organized communication. Also, at many points the patient's thoughts veer in new directions, apparently touched off by the stimuli and her own initial associations, but no longer governed by processes that maintain behavior consonant with environmental demands. We may refer to this as fluidity or looseness of association, but our attention is held to the implications for defects in ego functions that maintain surveillance and coordination over thought processes. The implication is that synthetic function does not alternately exist and fade but that momentary effectiveness is a brittle phenomenon that exists as a product of reactivity to environmental intrusion rather than as a product of synthetic function. Momentary stability is a reliance on this reactivity. At the point where a question is asked of the patient or a request made, the environment is much more actively intrusive than several seconds later when there is only the examiner sitting and waiting and the patient has some indistinct memory of what was asked and poor recollection of what she has been saying or thinking.

The character of the patient's "looseness" or fluidity varies with the degree of immediate environmental direction or guidance.

We may recall the discussion of this point in Chapter III. Tests vary in the nature of their directiveness, and this patient does very well on the Digits and Object Assembly subtests of the Wechsler. She is notably more fluid and introduces more irrelevancies in the Comprehension and Picture Arrangement subtests of this test and on other tests which, so to speak, open the gates for wider reaches of associations. The former tests, those in which she performs more adequately, are "closed systems" which define the elements to be dealt with and "tell" the patient how to deal with them; the latter tests merely introduce or open areas for reaction without offering delineating boundaries in which the patient is to operate. There are confusions on all tests, but it is predominantly in these "open-end" situations that the patient appears to violate situational requirements and to associate in a manner that suggests that her thoughts have lost their moorings with the original point of embarkation. At these moments ideas merge into new ideas without clear delineation. There is a changeableness in which perceptions appear to literally switch before the patient's eyes so that points of reference cannot be anchored and stability cannot be maintained. An illustration of this kind of instability and the patient's sense of experiencing confusion is seen in her comment to Rorschach Card VIII, "This looks like a fire, too, if it don't change." The manner in which such instability can yield not only to new thoughts but also to wider ranging ideas that veer out of control is expressed in her comments on Card IX, "Two prophets and a rainbow ... they are pointing toward the rainbow ... I think it means the end of the world, or the beginning of it." In these responses, the stimulus presented to the patient initiates a process of reality-based perception and conceptual association, but there is a lack of those governing processes that would bring the further associated elements into an organizational schema coordinated with the situational demand. In this panorama of functioning, the ego is not maintaining contact with reality demands and has concomitantly lost coordination of her mental processes.

ADAPTIVE CAPACITY AS A
FUNCTION OF STRUCTURE

In contrast to the previous patient, Mr. B, in whom we observed certain ego part processes which retained organization within concrete and narrow limits, the present patient shows elements of intactness of a different variety. Her areas of intact operation are far-flung rather than discrete and narrow. She is triggered into appropriate functioning by environmental intrusion and she can retain appropriateness if the effort is of short duration and if the processes of association are halted by external direction and by completion of effort. It is as though the continuity of a circumscribed effort itself may serve as the basis of continuity of ego functioning. Where such effort is not externally directed in terms of sharply delineated tasks or terminal points, the process loses direction and coordination.

In addition to the radical difference in style of functioning, the contrast between these two patients — both suffering synthetic function defect — has implications for differences in adaptive capacity. Mrs. K demonstrates very little in the way of ability to gear herself to the limitations of her defective structural system; one observes a gross helplessness in her functioning. It is as though outer stimuli have the impact power to get something started and what goes on continues only as long as that momentum can carry through a discrete set of mental processes. However, the impact effect wears off; what has been initiated within her carries on without coordination with the external and with no internal organization of the ensuing phenomena.

What this woman experiences must be inferred from an appraisal of the manner in which her processes function. She does, occasionally, develop discrete perceptions, conceptual organization, and interaction with reality and, at such time, we infer momentary experiences of integrity and identity as a psychological being. However, she also experiences the instability of such phenomena.

When mental processes race on in confusion, experience follows apace. She is lost in a stream of unbounded, ever changing groundless experiences that have an analogy in the constantly shifting kaleidoscope. In this context, the phenomenon of experience has lost its framework of organization — things happen, feelings come, antecedents are lost, contact with reality is disrupted, and sense of self in relation to environment is disintegrated. This is clearly a panic-producing condition and the patient reveals her distress and aimless struggle in frequent emotion-laden expressions of desperation.

TREATMENT POTENTIAL

The usual forms of psychotherapy would be of little use to this woman since they require prerequisites that this woman lacks: an organized ego capable of experiencing itself in relationship to another person, the capacity to accurately receive communications, and the capacity to gain conceptual perspective of oneself. This patient may be therapeutically engaged and greater adaptability fostered at the point where she has some capacity for reality contact and ego organization. With ego resources as weak and fluctuating as they are, therapy must embody forces of quality and quantity that will stimulate, arouse, hold, and reinforce ego reactions. Therapy must be concrete, physical, sensory, and directive. With DesLauriers, we recognize that therapy with severely regressed schizophrenics should initially focus on body experiences for the purpose of enchancing cathexis to body limits and heightening self-awareness directly. These recommendations suggest something other than traditional psychotherapy. Most of this kind of program can be carried out in a ward milieu, provided that ward personnel are consistent, resourceful, and ready to follow up the mechanical aspects of such a program with infusion of emotional meaningfulness (Colarelli and Siegel, 1966). Individual therapy may supplement this program in the form of a close, consistent relationship — consistent initially in time and space and with emphasis on amplification of open, direct communication from therapist to patient. This form of psychotherapy aimed at fostering ego strength is described in DesLaurier's approach to the treatment of chronic schizophrenics (1962).

TEST PROTOCOLS OF MRS. K

Wechsler-Bellevue I

	R.S.	Wt. S		
Inf.	12	9		
Com.	6-9	5-8		
Dig.	14	13		
Arith.	7	9		
Sim.	7-8	6-7		
Vocab.	18	8		
Verb.	50-54	42-45	Verbal IQ	94-98
P.A.	7-9	7-8	Perf. IQ	88-89
P.C.	9	8	Full Sc. IQ	90-93
Blks.	15	7		
Obj.	20	12		
Dig. S.	20	5		
Perf.		39-40		
Total		81-85		

Information

1.	Before – Dwight Eisenhower, oh, Truman.	1
2.	Therm – Something to take your temperature with.	1
3.	Rubber – Trees.	1
4.	London – In England.	1
5.	Pints – 2.	1
6.	Weeks – Um, (smiles) I don't know. Is it 48 weeks? Let's see – about 350, not right, huh, no it couldn't be.	0
7.	Italy – Athens.	0
8.	Heart – Pumps the blood through your body.	1
9.	Brazil – Africa – is that right? (laughs)	0
10.	Japan – Tokyo	1
11.	Plane – Wilbur and Orville Wright.	1

12.	Tall – 5'3", probably 5'6" – is it 5'6"? If I'm wrong, I'm wrong.	1
13.	Paris – Let's see, about 3 or 4 thousand miles – is that right?	1
14.	Hamlt – Shakespeare.	1
15.	Popn – I don't know – a million (laughs) I guess that one is wrong.	0
16.	Wash – Feb. the...12th.	0
17.	Pole – Leif Erikson.	0
18.	Egyp – In Israel, not right is it (laughs) maybe it is or it isn't. That wind is blowing like that...	0
19.	Finn – Mark Twain.	1
20.	Vati – Some kind of a vapor.	0
21.	Kora – Ain't got nothing to do with your blood, huh. I know that's wrong (laughs).	0
22.	Faust – I never heard of it. It's probably a book. Who wrote it? I don't know.	0
23.	Corp – A death certificate, or no a dead body, when a person dies.	0
24.	Ethn – Don't know. Something to do with chemicals.	0
25.	Apoc – Don't know.	0
	Score	12

Comprehension

1.	Env – Will take it to the post office.	2
2.	Thea – I don't know. Go to the (laughs) well, let's see. Go to the manager. Sure shouldn't holler fire. That's probably it, don't holler fire.	0-2
3.	B.C. – Cause it's bad for our morale. (?) Well, it's the way it affects our future life.	0-1
4.	Tax – I don't know (laughs) Well, to keep the government going or running.	2
5.	Shoe – Well, I don't know, go on – Is it because they are the longest for wear and tear?	1
6.	Land – I don't know that one – unless I think of it (smiles)–let's see. No, I can't think.	0
7.	For – Let's see. ... I don't know. In the daytime. Let's skip that one.	0
8.	Law – Let's see – to keep the people from going out of control. Can't answer those good.	1

9.	Mar – Well, I don't know (laughs) has it to, uh, so we won't, we can't have more than one wife, I guess.	0
10.	Deaf – Uh, I'll get it yet. Let me see. How do you write everything down. Let me see now. I can't think now.	0
	Score	6-9

Arithmetic

1.	4 + 5? (1″) $9.	1
2.	6c - 10? (1″) 4c Those are easy. Wait till we get to the hard ones.	1
3.	8c - 25? (3″) 17.	1
4.	or 36, or 4? (1″9).	1
5.	2 hrs 24 mi, 3 mph (2″) 8 hrs.	1
6.	7, 2c-50? (12″) 36.	1
7.	7 lb., 25, $1? (16″) 4, or wait a minute, 28 lbs.	1
8.	2/3 new, 400? – That's going to be a hard one, to figure in my head. I'm not through. Be $1200, don't know. 2/3 of 400. That's what you said.	
9.	(74″) Why do I have to do that (read) Don't know (solve it) I don't know. 30 ft. Pretty long, huh?	
10.	(79″) No, I don't know. Hum, I can't think on that one. I should know that right away.	
	Score	7

Similarities

1.	Or-Ba – I don't know. Isn't pollydrame. I read it. Or is it citrus?	0
2.	Ct-Dr – Both cloth and both clothing.	2
3.	Dg-Ln – Well, they're both four-footed.	1
4.	Wn-Bi – Uh, that one. I had a dream about a bicycle not very long ago. Both means of transportation. Both free wheeling but have to pump a bicycle.	1-2
5.	Pa-Ra – Both bring us the news.	1
6.	Ar-Wr – Go on to the next one. Something to do with 0, information. Don't write down everything I say. Guess it's okay.	1
7.	Wo-Al – I'll get it pretty soon. Well, that's a hard one. No – don't know that one. Go on.	0
8.	Ey-Er – I'll get those yet. Huh. Well, they're both sensitive to the mind. Sensations.	0

9.	Eg-Sd – They're both productive. (?) I mean, they multiply, don't they?	1
10.	Po-St – Well, I don't know. They both live forever.	0
11.	Pr-Pu – I guess I shouldn't be laughing. I was a scholar in school. Well, that one ought to be easy for me anyway. Well, Let's see. Oh dear, it's not. Oh, dear. Don't write that down.	0
12.	Fl-Tr – No, I don't. They don't sound alike, but they could be. Well, a fly is a . . . why don't you tell me.	0

Score   <u>7-8</u>

Picture Completion

1.	Gl – Bridge of the nose.	1
2.	Mn – The left mustache or right one.	1
3.	Mn – The car.	1
4.	Cd – There's one in the middle.	1
5.	Cr – What is that? Looks like a crab. Well, the head.	0
6.	Pg – Tail.	1
7.	Bt – The middle stem or upper most.	0
8.	Dr – Door knob.	1
9.	Wch – The second_____ .	1
10.	Pchr – Well, is the_____water in the glass already.	0
11.	Mr. – The other, sure right there.	0
12.	Mn – The necktie.	1
13.	Blb – The inner socket.	0
14.	Gl – Eyebrows.	1
15.	Sh – Handle to the cane.	0

Score   <u>9</u>

Picture Arrangement

Hse	6″	PAT	2	He's building a house.
Hold	16″	ABCD	2	Well, he's the man who committed a crime and is arrested, I guess.
Elev	28″	LMNO	2	Well, because the king's going up in the elevator.

Flirt	35″	JNETA 0-2 AJNET	Oh, he is going for a ride, sees that woman, gets out and goes with her. This should go first (A) but I'll leave it.
Fish	104″	EGFHJI 0	Well, little king went fishing and he caught two fish and that man in the water, or is that a man, then he goes down and king hollers at him.
Taxi	49″	SALMEU 1	He's got a bust of a woman. Hails a cab. She's on one side and he pulls her over to him and then he looks back once and looks back again.

Score $\overline{7\text{-}9}$

Block Design

A.   +

B.   + (With help)

1.   20″ + 3

2.   24″ + 3

3.   27″ + 3

4.   57″ + 3   I got all those to do yet.

5.   98″ + 3   Why do you make me do this — I'd better hurry up.

6.   210″ + 0   I can't figure this out. Is that right?

7.   425″ + 0   I think I'll quit for today. (Makes 1/4) That's all I'm going to make.

Score $\overline{15}$

Object Assembly

M	25″	6	A girl, no a boy.
Pr	39″	6/8	I know this a woman, but is she going to stay a woman. I hope she don't turn into a man. You don't know what that means, but I do. (ear backwards - but changes)
H	110″	6	Gets thumb, then takes other pieces in her hand. This is a hand, isn't it?

Score   20
_____

Vocabulary

1. App — Fruit.   1
2. Don — An animal, a mule.   1
3. Joi — Put together.   1
4. Dia — Stone, rare stone.   1
5. Nui — A bother (laughs).   1
6. Fur — That's a coat.   1
7. Cus — Seat.   1
8. Shi — Coin — it's in England.   1
9. Gam — Take a chance.   1
10. Bac — It's meat. Is it a pig's meat?   1
11. Nai — Why? It's a stay together, no, I don't know.   0
12. Ced — A tree.   1
13. Tin — That's a dye.   1
14. Arm — Well, I don't know, that's some kind of armor.   0
15. Fab — Fiction.   1
16. Bri — Full.   0
17. Gui — Uh, death sentence, well, I don't know.   ½
18. Plu — More than one.   1
19. Sec — Take away.   ½
20. Nit — Acid.   0
21. Sta — A verse.   1
22. Mic — Looking glass, the sky.   0
23. Ves — I've heard it, but, microscope is a lens.   0
24. Bel — Church steeple. I'm going all wrong today.   ½
25. Rec — Put back.   0
26. Aff — Oh, a disease.   ½
27. Pew — Powder.   0

28.	Bal – A vote.	0
29.	Cat – Kind of a_____	0
30.	Spa – Star.	0
31.	Esp – Oh, that's spy.	½
32.	Imm – That's right away, isn't it?	1
33.	Man – Don't know.	0
34.	Har – Suicide.	½
35.	Cha – That's a kettle.	0
36.	Dil – Lab.	0
37.	Ama – Don't know.	0
38.	Pro – Oh, I don't know.	0
39.	Moi – Don't know.	0
40.	Ase – Don't know.	0
41.	Flo – Don't know.	0
42.	Tra – Don't know.	0

Score   18-19

BRL Sorting Test

PART I

STIMULUS OBJECT	SORT AND VERBALIZATION	SCORE
Eraser (Free Choice)	<u>Ball</u>, <u>cork</u> ("Why do these objects belong together?") With my eyes closed? You mean anything that's made of the same thing? (Further encouraged) Aren't they all made of rubber?	 CD (L) (N)
Pipe	<u>Hammer</u>, <u>little screwdriver</u> (Q) Well, just all seem to go together. (Why) Cause they look like they belong together. I don't know, because I put 'em that way.	 (Arbitrary) Fail

Toy pliers	Bell, lock Cause I put 'em together, but I shouldn't.	(Arbitrary) Fail
Ball	Block, disk I did already. Cause, I don't know. I don't have a reason, just seemed they did like before.	 (Arbitrary) Fail
Fork	Knife, spoon, little silverware. Oh, I don't know. Well, first the big and then the little. Isn't that the way it's supposed to be? (Note adequacy of sort and subsequent loss of concept)	 (CD) S/N
Paper disk	Sink stopper, sugar cubes Cause I put 'em together. Well, I don't know. Two red and two white.	(Arbitrary) S/N Fail
Bell	Nothing	Fail

PART II

SORT	VERBALIZATION	SCORE
Smoking	All used for the same purpose — (Q) smoking.	FD
Metal	They're all made of metal, aren't they?	CD
Round	Well, the cigarette don't belong. Well, I don't know. Well, I don't know this one.	Fail
Tools	Some kind of a tool.	CD
Paper	Three red and two something else. I don't know about those two. Well, they could, if this belonged together they could. If it works out that way.	(Arbitrary) Fail

Doubles	Well, it's all what we use in our everyday living.	Syn
Red	They're all used for a purpose, for to work or for to play.	Syn S/N
Silverware	Uh, all eating utensils.	CD
Rubber	Rubber.	CD
White	Well, all white except one. (cigarette)	CD
Toys	Well, they would all go together. These there don't belong, not the same color.	Fail
Rectangles	I don't know that one. All blocks; well, square.	CD

Rorschach Protocol

FREE RESPONDING	INQUIRY

I.   20″   1. Looks like a bird, that's all.
              2. Oh well, two hands there. Do I have to tell everything I see?
              3. Two men
              4. And this looks like the back of a woman. That's all I see on that one.
      90″

1. The whole thing. Had wings. It looks like any bird in part. (Q) Uh, uh, flying. Don't it to you? W F M + A P
2. Shape. d 3 F + Hd
3. Chin or just the head or neck. Is there a head there or not? d7 F + Hd
4. Hips, feet, and part of arms. Hasn't got a head. Just the shape. Just part of her back. D4 F - Hd

II.   10″   1. That looks like two bears.
              2. That I don't know. That looks like some kind of bird down there too. That looks like two rocks; I don't know.

1. Well, just shape of bears, way they are standing. This one has his face toward that one, just putting their hands together. Let's hurry with this. W FM + AP
2. Then everything looks like a woman to me. (Q) Nothing, No,

3. Two hands there,
they're together there.
75" That's all I see.

not any. (Q) The shape, rocks.
D 1 F N
3. d1 F + Hd

III.   15"   1. Two bearded men right
there. What does it look
like to you? I don't like
to do this. Well nothing.
It looks like they're
warming their hands over
a fire.
2. There that looks like
somebody with them,
feet up in the air, to me.
80"   That's all I see.

1. That's the fire too, both.
Just bearded men. There and
there. (Beards) Can't you see it.
Fire - it looks like it, but seems
like they're warming their
hands. (Q) No, cause it's red.
W M, C H, Fire
(Fab. comb.)
2. Looks like a man, head,
back, feet. (Q) No. D2 F + H

IV.   71"   1. Well, that looks like a
man too, with his back
turned or what. A woman,
she's in, no, he's . . . this is
him and she's . . . I don't
know if she's in front or
in back. That's all I see.
125"   Two arms hanging down.

1. Well, he's standing over the
body of a woman. There's her
feet, otherwise she looks like
she has a gown on. Head, no,
I can't. (Q) At first she looked
like she was standing. She's
standing. (Q) No. Well, in one
way looks like he's just killed
her, but in another way, it
don't. D W F - H

V.   24"   1. Another one looks like
a bird too; everything
looks like a bird today.
2. Well, a little girl's feet
up there.
3. A crow's big claws
here.
91"   That's all.

1. Well, it's got wings - a back
there. (Q) No, I don't. Standing
still. W F + A P
2. Legs and feet. (Q) Well, if I
looked at it   long enough, the
head, (Q) No, I don't.
d3 F + Hd
3. Here, just looks like it.
d1 F + Ad

VI.   90"   1. That looks like a, oh
dear, I don't want to.
Well, looks like a . . . huh
. . . at first it looks like
Jesus.

1. Well, here and here. On the
cross. Well, while ago I could,
but now I can't. I want to go
back, it upsets me. D2 F + H
2. Forehead, nose, mouth,

2. Then when I ... There, that's all it looks like. Down at the bottom I don't know what it looks like. Looks like a man's face with a big nose.
214″ That's all.

eye, got its mouth open.
D1 F + Hd

VII. 36″ 1. That looks like something, something somebody fell into. I don't know what it would be. That's all it looks like.
2. Two chairs.
90″ That's all I see.

1. Well, looks about like a kettle or a volcano. First looked like a volcano, then looked different. Kettle - now, a kettle you cook something. W F - Obj.
2. Just chairs. They look a little like a throne, like a king sets on. Majestic, I'd say. D3 F - Obj.

VIII. 35″ 1. Hm − two wolves, red ones, you see 'em, or dogs. That's all.
2. This looks like a fire too, if it don't change.
3. Looks like the ribs of a man there.
125″ That's all.

1. Well, shape, pink (um, um). Well, I don't know, guess it did (Pink) They're standing on something. D 1 F(C) A(P)
2. There - well, it's red. D 7 C Fire
3. D 5 F + At

IX. 60″ 1. Oh, that, that's something else again. Let me see − that looks like two prophets. And a rainbow, you can see it. That looks like nothing, same old thing.
2. This looks like Statue of Liberty but it's across the water. Did it change again?
3. Two green dogs. Let's not say that.
4. Looks like some kind of men too.
5. And two angels there.
229″ That's all I see in there.

1. Here, just looks like it. Oh, they are pointing toward the rainbow. Yes, I think it means the end of the world, or the beginning of it. If everybody gets saved it's the beginning. Just because it was there with the prophets. It looks like a fire. I hope it changes though. It's going to be that if it don't change. Just does. D2+d3 M, F. H, Nat (Confab.)
2. Statue there. There's the frame. It is across the water. D8 F - (H)
3. I changed that. No D1 F - A
4. Head of a man. No, it looks

like it has horns. Devil somewhat. He's just there. D4 F+(Hd)
5. (Q) I didn't say angels. I
better quit what I'm doing.
(Q) There and there. Looks
like they're flying. Shape
mostly. S(tiny) M - (H)

X.   30" Well nothing.
            1. Two green dragons.
            2. This is a little girl's
            feet. I'm pointing it out,
            so you don't have to ask.
            I thought I was going to
            do different today.
            3. That red don't look
            like fire, not this time.
            Maybe it should. In one
            way it looks like old
            man fire.
      244" That's all.

1. Well, in shape of dragons – to
me, holding that little girl up.
(D7) You think this is going to
help you figure me out, do you.
Just her legs and dress. If she
lets them hold her, they will; if
she don't, they won't.
D1 FC A;
D7 F - Hd (Fab. comb.)
3. Here and here, you know
where that's at. Got a face
again, and he's red like fire.
D9 CF - (H), Fire (Contam.)

TAT

1. Let's see, I don't know. Well, that little boy is a concentrating
on whether he ought to take his violin lesson or not. Well, I don't
know. (Do) Well, I don't feel good. I think, I don't think that he
will. (Feel) Well, he feels like he don't care. (Thinking about) Well,
I think I'm, well he for a while he looked like my husband, then
it changed again. Well, he's thinking about the troubles he's got,
not troubles, of what somebody tried to tell him and he didn't
want to believe it. (What) Well, just... Oh, it was just, I don't
know, something to do with . . . it's gone now. It had something
to do with, I can't get it now. I can't concentrate.

2. Well, that, the man is plowing a field and the woman is, hum,
hum, she's reading the Bible, I guess, and that one is praying is
what she's doing. (Related) Maybe if I quit doing what I'm doing I
could concentrate. He don't talk (devil) to me. I just talk to

myself. Well, I don't know. (Happen) Well, I think if this was . . . I don't know. I think that that's the one, she would like to be his wife but that one is his wife. Well, I think this one lets it come to past . . . this one will become his wife. If she don't follow the right path instead of the wrong one. I hope she follows the right one. Do you? You think she won't. You're not so dumb. You're smart. I think she will follow the right.

3 GF. That's a woman crying in the, I was going to say fear. That's all I'm going to say because it's all I know. It could be shame and sometimes it's fear. (Afraid of) Herself, because she, just because she didn't listen. She doesn't know if she's going to take the right path or wrong one. Shame is when she didn't listen, like said last night. She's always walking up and down; put one foot in front of the other, crying or laughing. You know, that girl Patsy. Visions of Patsy and herself.

4. I don't know. I'm not going to tell no more. Looks just like a man and a woman. Well, he wants to go someplace but she doesn't want him to. (Go) No, I don't know. She will if she has a strong enough will to do. I hope so.

6 GF. Well, I tell you. I can't do any more today. Oh, shoot, I don't know. Can't even think. Looks like his daughter or is it his wife. I'm through. I'm too mad today at myself. I won't talk. Let's see — I wouldn't — I don't feel good today. That's my sin. I don't know. Well, sure. Well, I don't know. She's sitting there. I don't know what she's doing and he's talking to her. (Saying) Something about, I don't know. I can't make it up today. About how, I wouldn't know. Don't write everything down. That won't help you to understand me.

7 GF. Oh, the, this is about a mother and her daughter. She's reading. (Reading) Well, the Bible, I think. (Feel) Well, she feels sad. Looks like it, or is it not, or if it is it's wistful. (Happen) I

don't know. (Thinking) I don't know. Thinking about what her mother is reading to her.

9 GF. How many we got? I don't like to tell 'em. Well, this is a, I don't know. I can't, we can wait three weeks from now. She's running away from something and she's watching her, going down the river, isn't she? Well, I had a, this one had something in her hand. Is it a shirt? Looks like a shirt today. (Away from) Is that all? I told you herself. Cause she, uh, found that she went too far, I guess. (In what) Just too far, maybe. (Watching her) She wants her to come back, I guess. Her sister.

10.   What did you do yesterday between 1:00 and 2:00. I wasn't on the ward. This looks like a . . . I have to quit listening to that devil. Looks like a father and mother, or is it a mother and father. Well, she's trying to console him. (What) I don't know, about their future, I guess.

12 F. Oh, dear, that looks like me there (hag). Oh, she looks like, she, I don't know what this is. That's life and that's life (hag) and that's death (girl). Happening. Well, that's all it looks like. I want to hurry up and get over this. She's afraid and she isn't (hag) but yet, oh, just people don't like to die, do they?

12 M. That's a man trying to make his son well. (How) By, you know, sometimes I think one way sometimes, and sometimes I think another. I tell you, I mean he's praying. (Well) It doesn't look like it, but he will, but he might. I hope he does. (Wrong) I don't know. I think he's spiritually misguided or something?

13 MF. Oh, we only got two more. I don't know. I don't act this way on the ward. Listen! Don't write this down. Looks, um, he's sorry because he killed her. (Why) I don't know. (Laughs) Well, I don't know. (Happen) Well, why do I think he killed her? Well, let see, he's, uh, he didn't want to admit what he done. (Done) Well like the, like that woman said, he had been immoral. Last night an

old woman told me a story like this. (Happen) If she don't, I don't know. Well, I think it will if she doesn't put the blame on herself cause then it would look like she committed suicide, but she didn't.

18 GF. One More — Oh, let's see. Looks like a body has fallen down the stairs and she tried to pick him back up. She did. Does everybody look at these same pictures? (Happened) Well, she really went up the stairs first and he tried to follow her and fell. Well, just like that, a dream my little girl had. There's a little boy and a little girl and the boy fell down the stairs and he couldn't get up. His eyes, he looks like he was sleeping. (Dead) Well, I don't, I don't, well, he does look like it there, don't he? (Feel) Sorry.

CHAPTER VII

Mr. D: Vacillation Between Reality and Psychosis

A few weeks before testing, this patient had developed an acute psychosis. Previously a respected professional man and "pillar" of his community, he had, to outward appearances, suddenly developed ideas of persecution. He had armed himself and fled in panic in his car. Two days later, confused and in terror, he arrived at his parents' home in the next state. Hostility, paranoid thinking, fearfulness, and flight of ideas were the predominant symptoms in the first two weeks of hospitalization. With continued medication and a more directive approach on the part of personnel, he rapidly became more lucid and hyperactivity receded. The main questions asked of the psychological examination, which was completed during the third week of hospitalization, concerned recommendations for treatment subsequent to the patient's "remission."

This case was chosen as an illustration of lack of ego synthesis where functioning occurs on the periphery of reality with consequent intense struggles as the patient works toward integration but frequently lapses into borderline confusion. There are elements that overlap with our other cases: this man can find stability in highly structured reality just as we observed in the functioning of Mr. B; he lapses into helpless disorganization as did Mrs. K; he works toward forcing reality data into a pseudo-reality organization, although in this endeavor he falls short of the success that Mr. P, our final case, achieves by this method. Mr. D's test protocols are reproduced beginning on page 134.

ORGANIZATION AS A FUNCTION OF
ENVIRONMENTAL DIRECTION

The test responses present a pattern of fluctuation but with some intervals of adequate functioning. These occur in such a manner that, if we had only a limited sample of those intervals, we might infer contact with reality, organized ego processes, and the apparent experience of intactness — in short, an intact synthetic function. However, at other moments our behavior samples contradict this impression and the patient's functioning breaks down in all three areas of synthetic functioning: the patient's behavior or expressions appear rather divorced from the task; the ego processes themselves lose coherence and organization; and there is evidence that the patient experiences loss of a phenomenal feeling of intactness. It is important to trace the factors involved in this divergence in order to reconstruct a picture of the ego structure involved.

This pattern of divergence falls into sub-groupings with special characteristics. Although apparent at many points in testing, this divergence is especially clear under varying conditions of external structure as illustrated by the comparison of his functioning on the two portions of the BRL Sorting test. As described earlier, in the *active* part the patient is required to "venture forth" and develop a system of organization with but one object as a starting point. He must create organization through analysis of possible concepts of similarity and difference. He must utilize judgment and reality appraisal in deciding on "appropriate" groupings. What we mean by "appropriate" is the judging of what might be consensually accepted by others, for the task essentially involves the communication of one's rationale to another person, the examiner. This implies judgment based on experience in one's culture and involves the accruing of knowledge of what is accepted and what serves the purposes of reality adjustment. In the passive portion, the subject has the task of recognition — fitting concepts to already structured data; he must find the conceptual category that "best fits" the sorting presented to him. This requires screening, testing his products against input information, and again judging what he produces via reality testing processes.

In the active portion of the Sorting Test, our patient responds hesitantly; he appears to grope for appropriate concepts; and he conveys his conclusions in uncertain terms. For example, he prefaces three groupings with such expressions as "I suppose," "I assume," "I don't know." On item 1 he verbalizes his thoughts as he considers whether the objects placed with the screwdriver (the toy tools, pliers, nails, and block) are tools, belong in a workshop, or are used for play. His thinking reflects the vacillation in his efforts to decide on a basis for grouping: to item 4, the ball, he responds by adding the sink stopper, real cigar, pipe, bell, paper disk, and corks and then quibbles about the roundness and redness and the necessity for drawing "a line somewhere" even though "they are matters of little importance." The answers that he gives may be characterized as syncretistic and arbitrary; they create categories but fail to relate to outstanding attributes intrinsic to the objects. In addition, the patient appears unable to reappraise his responses to gain some perspective of where they fail although he has a sense of missing the mark: "Each time you have to have some kind of rule and what rule you use doesn't make any difference as far as I can see." In contrast, in the passive portion of this test he gives the appearance of an intact, efficient, and intelligent person; he responds briefly, to the point, and with some indications of awareness of the appropriateness of his responses.

The difference in adequacy of functioning characterizing these two portions of the Sorting Test provides a key to analyzing the patient's ego functions. We are led to suspect that the problem centers on the comparative requirements that these two tasks place on the ego processes of the patient. The evidence points toward the active portions as a challenge sufficient to overtax ego processes and to reveal flaws in functioning. Evidence from other tests helps clarify this aspect. At several points on the Wechsler, especially where the subtests foster conditions of clarity and directness as to what is required, the patient functions well. On the Arithmetic subtest his answers are quick and fairly accurate. The same is true for Picture Completion and for the placement order of cards of Picture Arrangement. These tasks are relatively clearly delineated. The data to be worked with are before the subject in their entirety and it is clear that he is to work with what is before him. However, his functioning is different when the task departs from this delimited structure and demands of the patient that he deal with the situation in whatever way he judges best and with whatever thoughts that come. Under these conditions we observe a progressive process in which functioning begins at a point of close relationship to stimulus material and digresses further and further from it. When he seeks the similarity of coat and dress, he begins with "both garments" but goes on with, "hide your nakedness." Dog and lion are given as "both animals," but then, "capable of killing with their physical bodies."

Illustrations from the Rorschach demonstrate the same progression of greater remoteness from the reality properties of the tasks. The patient's starting point on each card bears relatively close relationship to blot properties, but, as he proceeds, his responses appear to be governed less by such properties. The progression on Card I is: ancient bird, ugliness, my children having fun at home with bright colors. On Card II the sequence is: vertebrae in back, bloody operation for removal of tissues in back, ugliness, flower that could be saved or lost to blight. And, on Card III: people sitting at a table, discussion of some vile or evil subject because of the symbolic blood stain. In each sequence one can seek to understand the significance of the material that intrudes; a more critical point of concern, however, is the nature of the failure of ego processes that is being revealed and the extrapolation of inferences about this patient's ego functioning in extra-test situations.

RELATIONSHIP BETWEEN LOSS OF REALITY CONTACT
AND INNER CONFUSION

These phenomena illustrate a progressive loss of interaction and coordination with the material to which the patient is presumably responding. Like Mrs. K, he starts at a point where reality prompts him and if reality affords the opportunity to cling closely and bind his functioning to what is concretely present, ego processes maintain contact and internal organization. In this respect, Mr. D also resembles Mr. B but the difference, of course, is that Mr. D does not maintain the close, concrete constriction to available data. Mr. B mechanically clung to the concrete immediacy of stimuli. In this test record, Mr. D shows no such constriction. It is as though he maintains contact only so long as reality extends a forceful hand to him, but if reality presents itself non-intrusively and leaves him to handle the task of continual testing-out and relating himself to the environment, he loses his relationship to reality.

What has been described is a serious limitation of the patient's capacity to maintain his reality testing and synchronization with reality data. It is small wonder that contact is such a fragile phenomenon, and in this quality we recall our observations of Mrs. K. In both of these cases this particular aspect is quite similar: there is a passive helplessness in the individual's capacity to develop some pattern of functioning directed toward liaison with the external.

In the psychoanalytic framework, loss of contact with reality is conceptualized as a weakening of cathexis to ego boundaries and a withdrawal or loss of cathexis to object relationships. As this weakening and loss occurs, a series of ego failures ensue. Whether or not the psychoanalytic concepts are used, if we examine the patient's behavior at these points of loss of reality contact, we are able to reconstruct the structural events that are taking place. What occurs can be described at first generally and then in specific, illustrative detail. Initially, inner ideation interacts with reality data but, as the interaction weakens, ideation progressively governs thought processes in a direction increasingly foreign to reality considerations. Emotional components intrude but instead of being brought into synchronized, controlled relationships, they appear to pitch haphazardly in directions signaled by ideation. The patient's conceptual framework shifts erratically from one extreme to another, unable to stabilize at some judicial point. Language becomes stilted and stylistic and in relative isolation from other behavioral avenues. Finally, psychotic projection emerges.

In a sample of the patient's test behavior, we can trace these elements. Rorschach Card IX brings to the patient's mind the imagery of a small child's sloppiness. Rather than bringing such a conception into closer consonance with the stimulus (e.g., elements in the blot that create such an impression, or further delineation of the concept), emotion intrudes ("much happiness") along with an extraneous, apparently unrelated thought (concerning psychiatry and religion). The happiness theme is reversed, but the reversal is not an organized, considered, rationalized attitude but an intrusion whose source is lost to him. He can project that psychiatrists adulterate the picture presumably because the picture is experienced as evil and he is in the hands of psychiatrists. The thought, not sensed as his own mental working, is given credence as fact. At this point another reversal takes place and the picture can be conceived as beautiful. Perhaps a doubt entered his mind whether evilness was a correct interpretation; unable to consider and evaluate the relationship, the effort to find greater appropriateness results in the affect swinging to the opposite pole.

In the inquiry to the cards, yet another direction is sought and may have been an effort at avoiding disorganization. Instead of ideational and emotional havoc, there is an effort to cling to the blots, not in terms of perceptual creations that bring confusion, but in terms of concrete closeness almost to the sensory impressions. This is done critically as if criticism might be a tactic of hanging on to the stimulus: a part is "well laid out" or "smudged" or "blotted"; another part is "all fouled up and run together, not beautifully run together but in an adulterous sort of way." As the patient proceeds he again loses his grip on the concrete and injects that an adulterous act or an accident has occurred. When pressed he brings in concepts of symbolism and finally responds, "It reminds me of ideas running together."

What has occurred here reflects efforts to hold to reality but these efforts are ineffective and the patient easily loses his bearing on reality. His apparent questioning of extremes of affect lead him to opposites: good and bad, ugly and beautiful, but just as there is no basis for seizing on one extreme, the patient finds no grounding in the reverse extreme. Finally, as organization continues to lapse, he expresses his own momentary phenomenological experience of the situation: "It reminds me of ideas running together."

DISORGANIZATION AND THE EXPERIENCE OF LOSS OF ANCHORAGE

These phenomena have occurred under conditions which must be inferred as synthetic function absence or impairment. The ego processes that direct, guide, control, and channel mental phenomena are currently too weak and, in consequence, the patient lacks the concomitant experience of being able to follow what is occurring within him and to him. The confusion is at two levels: the disorganized mental events and the disorganized experience of those events. The patient cannot maintain distinction between ideas coming from within or from without and he cannot maintain a surveillance of what phenomena led to what result. An emotion prompted by some inner stimulus is experienced by itself with no locus of cause or effect and is consequently easily but arbitrarily located in external stimuli. There is no capacity to evaluate or redirect himself because he has lost his grounding in why he is going on. He desperately utilizes some efforts at definite organization such as seizing on conceptual extremes or locating the source of experience outside of himself (projection), but nothing is solid, nothing stays put, and mental events run on. He loses a sense of where he is because the mental events that provide such a groundwork have faltered.

THERAPEUTIC RECOMMENDATIONS

While clinical evidence of remission at the time of testing was strong, testing itself indicates that this process is far from complete. The contrast between evidence of his remarkable progress in the ward and his functioning under test conditions, involving reduced environmental structure or direction, indicates that this capacity should not be overestimated and his treatment program, which has been structural support and unambiguous directiveness, should be continued for a time. The test material shows that the intrusion of emotional and dynamic conflicts still leads toward progressive disorganization until the patient is rescued by elements of reality intrusion. We expect the same problem to be encountered in therapeutic efforts. This man quickly and easily pours out indications of his fears and concerns, so that the therapist may be enticed by what appears to be his readiness to examine internal dynamic problems. However, structural considerations suggest that this would be less than therapeutic for two reasons: (1) the patient's foremost problem is that of a weak ego that has demonstrated its capacity for disorganization, and (2) exploration of dynamic conflicts or unconscious or primary process problems taxes or disrupts the currently unstable organization of ego processes. Dealing with "depth" material or dynamics connotes communication between patient and therapist that focuses on disguised meaning, symbolism, non-manifest emotion, and other focus of covert expression. All of these are precisely the opposite of what the weakened ego is able to conceptually organize and experience, and the patient's efforts to grapple with communication on this level lead him to greater confusion. The recommendation, therefore, is for a milieu and psychotherapy program that permits the patient to strengthen those ego processes that facilitate reality contact and further inner integration. Psychotherapy should foster the patient's experience of who he is, what his relation is to the therapist, how his emotions can be recognized and realistically expressed in a reality oriented framework, how ideational intrusive ideas can be checked against reality and portions of them selectively utilized as they find some appropriate reality context. As this process develops, patient and therapist may direct attention to examining the conditions that disrupt the patient and the circumstances that provoke such distress in him that his ego cannot sustain an organized state. The goal is to prevent the recurrence of the patient's psychosis by helping him deal with his primary problem, that of maintaining reality contact and ego organization.

TEST PROTOCOLS OF MR. D

Wechsler-Bellevue I

	R.S.	Wt. S		
Inf.	23	16		
Com.	11-15	10-13		
Dig.	10-12	7-10	Verbal IQ	118-124
Arith.	10	13	Perf. IQ	105-121
Sim.	19	15	Full Scale IQ	113-125
P.A.	11-14	10-12		
P.C.	10-12	9-12		

Information

1. Before –   1
2. Therm – It's a scientific instrument that is designed to measure temperature of the day, or air or water, or anything else.   1
3. Rubber – Rubber tree plus some additives usually.   1
4. London – In England, British Isles.   1
5. Pints – 2 pints in a qt., 4 cups in a qt.   1
6. Weeks – 52.   1
7. Italy – Rome.   1

8.	Heart – Well, scientists presume it pumps blood through the system and also to lungs where it is aerated.	1
9.	Brazil – South America.	1
10.	Japan – Tokyo.	1
11.	Plane – Wright Brothers are supposed to have, but actually it was invented long before them – Leonardo da Vinci, for one.	1
12.	Tall – Don't have any idea for certain, but I suppose about 5′5″.	1
13.	Pairs – about 2000 miles.	1
14.	Hmlt – Shakespeare.	1
15.	Popn – 170,000,000 roughly, very roughly.	1
16.	Wash – Feb. 22.	1
17.	Pole – Well, that's a big question. Admiral Byrd is supposed to have first discovered it. It's been discovered ever since the beginning of the world, people have known it was there. If you mean who put the first flag up there, another guy is supposed to have been up there before Byrd.	1
18.	Egyp – It's at the southeast corner of the Mediterranean Sea – the northeast corner of Africa.	1
19.	Finn – Mark Twain.	1
20.	Vati – It's the geographical area set off for the Pope of the Catholic Church – for the government of the Catholic Church – next to or part of the city of Rome.	1
21.	Kora – It's the holy book of the Moslem religion.	1
22.	Faust – Not sure – I think that Shakespeare may have written that. I'm not positive – don't believe it was Shakespeare.	1
23.	Corp – Latin words meaning have the body and it is the name of a writ, oh, requires that a person who has a body in captivity to deliver that body in court – I could go on for hours about that.	0
24.	Ethn – Well, I don't know what it means – but from wording I assume it's study or knowledge about ethics – this sounds like one of those words that got made up by somebody for their own use and sooner or later got in the dictionary.	0
25.	Apoc – Portion of holy writing. Something attributed to Holy Bible or should be 6-8 or 10 books including some good ones – including particularly story of Suzanne.	1
	Score	23

Comprehension

1. Env – You're required by law to put it in the mailbox or deliver it to the postal authorities, and that's the thing to

do — unless it's addressed to you and then you should open the thing.   1-2

2. Thea — That would depend a great deal on the circumstances. You'd have to give the alarm some way — whatever the appropriate way was. (Q) Might be telling the manager, if you were close at hand to him. It wouldn't be screaming "fire," that's for sure.   1-2

3. B.C. — Well, I don't know as we necessarily should but long periods of association with bad company are likely to produce like characteristics in ourselves to the persons who are the bad company; short periods are not.   1-2

4. Tax — To support the government — pay for governmental services.   2

5. Shoe — Well, not always, but that's a good thing to make one out of. Protects one's feet while permitting air to enter to feet — mainly that's what we like (Q) Japanese like wood — my son likes tennis shoes made out of cloth and rubber — if we had to walk in 3″ water — rubber like shoe — it's appropriate to the circumstances when I . . .   0-1

6. Land — Because men value it more, and they value it more for many reasons — usually because it's served by public utilities and closer to market place and close to other people than don't like to be.   1

7. For — Well, I would try to get direction indication from piece of landscape or from sun or from growth of trees — moss on north side but hard to find. (Q—sun) As a direction indication. (Q) Sun is always a good distance indicator. (Q) Sun always moves in orbit across sky — essentially from east to west, but also swings to south in this latitude.   2

8. Law — Because men are not disposed to treat each other as they should without laws. (Q) Well, they do bad towards each other. Man's inhumanity to man may count as thousands more laws make men do to other men as they should — unsatisfactory for the purpose, but for the purpose.   1

9. Mar — Same answer as the last — why they do — state is arrogant in that it thinks, it thinks, it should require a license but that's the way it is so people should go along with it. (Arrogant) Well marriage is a religious matter and state has injected itself into matters of church at this point and church has permitted it, so it's okay — since it has happened centuries ago, no

	reason to overturn it − since it has been permitted for centuries.	0
10.	Deaf − Because it produces such an impediment to their communication that they have a difficult time learning how they should speak − actually they could learn.	2

Score   11-15

Arithmetic

1.	4 + 5 (1 ″) 9.	1
2.	6c - 10 (1 ″) 4.	1
3.	8c - 25 (1 ″) 17.	1
4.	or 36, or 4 (2 ″) 9.	1
5.	2 hrs 24 mi, 3 mph (2 ″) 8.	1
6.	7, 2c-50 (9 ″) 36.	1
7.	7 lb, 25, $1? (15 ″) about 20 (Q) 28.	0-1
8.	2/3 new, 400 (3 ″) $600.	1
9.	(46 ″) 22-1/2 unless you want to go over it again.	0
10.	(10 ″) 96 I guess.	3

Score   10

Picture Completion

1.	Gl − Man doesn't have any nose piece.	1
2.	Ln − Man's only got one-half of a mustache.	1
3.	Mn − Appears like the man is wearing lipstick and man has no ears.	0
4.	Cd − Nine of diamonds with eight spots. Nine of diamonds with eight spots − one spot missing.	1
5.	Cr − Crab with no front part of his head.	0
6.	Pg − Pig with no tail − can't tell if he's got an eye or not.	1
7.	Bt − Steamship with no smokestacks.	1
8.	Dr − Door with no door handle − but that's not too unusual.	0-1
9.	Wch − Second dial hasn't got a second hand on it and it's out of place for most watches.	1
10.	Pchr − Water isn't pouring out of pitcher.	1
11.	Mr − Guess chair and seat aren't there (r) That is bottom of chair and bottom of seat − and her image in mirror is not the same as that in front.	0-1

12.	Mn – Man with no buttons and no tie on the front of his shirt.		1
13.	Blb – No screws.		1
14.	Gl – Her lip isn't complete on this woman – hair isn't complete – but way it's sketched – her right eye _____ .		0
15.	Sh – Man doesn't have his shadow.		1

Score   10-12

Picture Arrangement

Hse	4″	PAT	2	Man is building, a house, painting it, finishing it.
Hold	8″	ABCD	2	
Elev	9″	LMNO	2	
Flirt	30″	AJNET	2	Little king riding in a Cadillac. Little king takes the package on his head and they walk down the street happily.
Taxi	55″	SAMUEL	3	This story could be told backwards or forwards maybe. Man walking down the street with the top part of a manikin; sees the taxi, motions it down, he gets in taxi and plays like he's loving his wife – slowly comes to his senses and puts it over. Could be told a second way. A man is apparently playing like he's loving a manikin in a car but appears to be a woman; someone observes him doing this and he notices it and gets upset and pushes the manikin over. We know it is a manikin but it appears to be a manikin, and he gets out of the car with the manikin and gets a taxi to go home or elsewhere (why gets out of car) feels guilty, been caught and feels guilty – can't
		MUESLA	(0)	enjoy himself anymore.

| Fish | 43″ | EFGHIJ | 3 | Little king apparently fishing; he catches one fish, then another fish, then since he has two fish he hollers down and servant comes up with another fish — been placing them on the hook — many morals could be drawn (Q) Height of stupidity and foolishness — not the way to fish. |

Score $\overline{11\text{-}14}$

BRL Sorting Test

PART I

STIMULUS OBJECT	SORT AND VERBALIZATION	SCORE
Screwdriver (Free choice)	Oh, that's a silly . . . I suppose you mean tools. Toy tools, <u>pliers</u>, <u>nails</u>, <u>block</u>. ("Why do they belong together?") Well, they're all . . . such matters as belong in a workshop or a play workshop – find 'em all in my workshop. Kids play with these things. As they get older, play with bigger . . . If I was a bachelor, wouldn't answer that way – suppose some other way.	CD → Syn 1
Pipe	<u>Real cigarette</u>, <u>candy cigarette</u>, <u>real cigar</u>, <u>toy cigar</u>, <u>matches</u>. (Q) Well, they're either smoking materials or the likes of smoking materials.	CD
Toy Pliers	Well, I assume you don't want me to go back and do what I did before and I assume you want me to do toys. Toy tools, toy silver-ware, <u>ball</u>, <u>bell</u>, <u>corks</u> (go in toys),	

pipe, block, paper forms, maybe a couple of marginal items like eraser and sugar lumps, real cigar. Couple of items I wouldn't give my kids (Q) real cigar and pipe. (Q) Suitable toys for children except these two, yet they are intended as toys. Exactly what a kid does when he gets a hold of block and nails . . . mine do.

CD → Fab
L

Ball

Well, I don't know. You could put these in several piles but could put everything that is round in its nature, particularly that is round and red also . . . red not enough, I don't think. Cigarettes wouldn't hardly . . . Stopper, real cigar, pipe, bell, paper disk, corks. This is red and round (rubber cigar) screwdriver is round and red too but it's essentially something else. This, of course, is nonsense, got to draw a line somewhere. (Q) Because round and because they essentially are round or essentially red and because they are matters of little importance and got to draw a line somewhere. Doubtful whether pipe fits but it's good and round. Besides cork fits in pipe.

CD → Arbitrary (L)

Fork

Spoon, knife, sugar, toy silverware, cigar, candy cigarette, matches, cigarette, stopper. (Q) Have to do with a meal.

Syn
L

Paper Disk

Paper square, index card. Could probably put everything down there because that's just a toy for a psychologist, but limiting it severely – these are paper items. Each time you got to

CD

	have some kind of a rule and what rule you use doesn't make any difference as far as I can see.	
Bell	Let's see . . . that's for an older boy. He would play with this kind of things. <u>Screwdriver, pliers</u>, eraser, <u>block, lock</u>. (Q) Well, the item you put down was bicycle or tricycle bell . . . anyway would have to be put on with a screwdriver and the boy that owned it would like to play with these other things including putting on a lock on his trike. If there's a marginal item, it would have to be a padlock.	Fab L

PART II

SORT	VERBALIZATION	SCORE
Smoking	All have to do with smoking. Either play or real.	CD
Metal	All metal.	CD
Round	All round essentially anyway.	CD
Tools	All sharp tools, play or real . . . or household tools, play or real.	CD
Paper	All essentially paper.	CD
Doubles	All pairs – one play and one real . . . except some there like sugar, cardboard, nails. . .all pairs anyway.	CD
Red	All red essentially.	CD
Silverware	All utensils for eating food – play or real.	CD (S/N)

Rubber	All rubber ... also all red.	CD
White	All white, essentially again.	CD
Toys	All toys, theoretically. (Q) Cigar certainly not an appropriate toy, nevertheless, it's regarded as one.	CD
Rectangles	Well, they're all essentially vegetable matter, all essentially manufactured items, and they're all essentially dirty, and all squares essentially ... probably some other reasons.	SYN→CD

Rorschach Protocol

FREE RESPONDING	INQUIRY

I.

5″   1. Well, it reminds me somewhat of an ancient bird, somewhat.
2. Also of a vertebra in the back.
3. Also a crab.
Reminds me of ugliness of course. And also reminds me of my children at home – having fun at home with bright
40″   colors – doing this sort of thing – they will all, no doubt remind me of that.

1. (see) Well, the color and wings sticking out and the body and face. I can't think of the name of it, but I mean a pre-historic bird – (position) headed away from me. I'm looking down at top or up at bottom – probably down.
W FC + A P
2. Crease in the paper – apparent crease. (Q) Oh, this whole thing has the appearance of a vertebra in the back. If you had pictures I could show you which one – or which ones.
W F + At
3. (Describe) Well, the wings are claws instead of wings headed away from me or I'm looking down on it, or he's standing up on hind

legs and looking toward
me or I'm looking toward
him – crabs do that, by the
way. Very interesting
people.
W FM A

II.

5 "   1. This also reminds me also
of vertebra in back.
2. Also of a very bloody
operation for removal of
tissue in back – seen in a
movie once.
Also of ugliness.
3. And with terrific imagination, see a flower that
could be saved here – or one
that has just been lost to
blight.

1. (Describe) Spinal cord
goes up inside. Red doesn't
have anything to do with it
unless you think of it being
obstructed from person's
back.
W F + (CF) At, B1
2. Saw a picture once of an
extraction of a ruptured
disc – bloody thing – only
time I can ever remember
that a picture made me sick
to my stomach. I wasn't
alone either. (Q) That picture show, but also some-
thing bloody – something
bloody – something cut
up – not like a steak – but
more like uh – a run over
animal or something
like that.
W CF - At
3. Pods something like a
poppy – one that has been
blighted (impression) black-
ness, redness that shows
through.
D₁ FC- P1

III.

10 "   This reminds me to some
extent of two people sitting
at a table – by use of considerable imagination, of
course – probably having a

discussion of some vile subject or evil subject the symbolic blood stain and be-
cause of the symbolic black
color and because of evil
faces. Conspirators I suppose you would say.

DW M, FC , CF, H, B1
(Sym)

1'20"

If it weren't so homely it
would remind me of happy
games, or my wife and I
sitting at coffee talking
over what happened today,
but those are always
2'0"   pleasant and this is not.

IV.

8 "   1. This would look a little
like a crocodile or some other
monster crawling out from
under a ledge or a tree trunk,
and probably in a dense forest
area – reminds me of South
America – Dakar, Africa.
Also because of its ugliness
reminds me of bad things instead of good things.
2. Might, if it weren't so ugly,
remind me of a cow eating
vegetation – but it don't –
too ugly – yet if you look at
something hard enough, the
ugly can be beautiful too –
2'10"   particularly if you get used
to it. In fact, it reminds me
of (patient's name) – who if
you're around him long
enough, is a pretty nice boy,
but has a look as ugly as
3'08"   anything – fine young man.

1. He's headed toward
me – here's his two eyes and
here's his snout – and rest of
him is back underneath
this – except this could be
two front legs, and this
could be something cover-
ing him, possibly like a
backdrop of forest – under-
brush – and this is probably
suggesting these limbs – in
other words picture bends
in the middle - upper part is
vertical and lower part is
horizontal.
DW FM- A
2. Some head – this is hard
to imagine – but it's got
kinda dumb, peaceful look
to it like that.
DW FM- Ad

V.

7 ''   Well, this one is not so ugly –
        it could be a butterfly or it
        could be a bat, being black
        it's probably meant to be a   W FC + A P
        bat, but it's too delicately
        done to be anything very
        hideous – probably meant
60 ''   to be a butterfly.

VI.

6 ''   1. This could be a polar bear   W F+ A, obj (P)
        rug, or a . . .   2. Q – Well, you would have
        2. Tiger slinking through the   to be above the tiger – look-
        woods and would remind me   ing straight down at it –
        of nonsense and foolishness   head at top – whiskers
        mainly.   sticking out at side – ears
                                           and little shaggies out
                                           along throat – sleekness
                                           suggests its being a tiger
                                           and fact that colors have
                                           arranged themselves like
                                           tiger stripes not very much
                                           – and _____ suggests
                                           roundness – doesn't have
                                           any tail.
50 ''   W FM, Fc- A

VII.

8 ''   Oh, this card reminds me of
        vertically formed clouds but
        it's not a good representation
        of them – or something light
        and fluffy like cotton piled
        up on top of each other and
        balanced.   W KF C1
        It's balanced and is a lighter
        color and . . . probably has a
        good meaning rather than
1'16'' a bad one.
1'25'' It's more artistic than the rest.

VIII.

4 "

1. This picture reminds me of my vacation last summer – in oh we looked at the beautiful stones at   – and of color, reminds me of much happiness – its colors are bright and delicate and makes me think of happy things.

W   CF-   N

2. I can see two animals that are not very vicious looking – friendly animals climbing up the side — and a uniquely planted tree at the top – not planned but manifested – it's symmetrically balanced.

(Kind of animals) Oh, chipmunks or groundhogs or puppy dogs- possibly real tame bears like they have in Yellowstone – baby bears or teddy bears (2) pandas, something like that. (pos) crawling up the side – head toward top; feet - two of feet toward bottom – as if crawling up on the side of the picture – or like a groundhog sitting up, looking around outside of its hole.

1'45"

D1   FM+   A P
D3   F   P1

IX.

8 "

This one is also with bright colors but it's sloppy and it reminds me of a very small child having done it, but with much happiness.

It also reminds me of psychiatrists attempting to handle religious matters in which they know nothing about and adulterates the whole picture. Yet I see that if this was changed but just a little it would be the most beautiful one of all of them.

(Q) Well, at bottom is well laid out pink area that is not smudged or blotted and at top also not smudged or blotted and green also – but in middle all fouled up, all run together – and not beautifully run together but in an adulterous sort of way – more like it had been by accident – an unhappy accident. (Q) This is symbolic – it reminds me of that – instead of crea-

tures or physical sub-
stances, it reminds me of
ideas running together.
W C   Sym Abs

1'40"

X.

8"   1. This one has somewhat
of an oriental appearance to
me – use of many bright
colors and fine sense of
artistry – well balanced –
colors are well blanded –
but too spotty. Looks like   W   C   Art
it's something that's been
done by somebody that had
thoughts that were too
scattered out, and yet it's
very attractive – probably
done by a woman.

1'15" (See anything in this)
...I can see a flower but   There's a flower called the
it's a rare flower that I   Bird of Paradise which is
haven't seen in a long time   most colorful – have to turn
and haven't really seen any-   it over or think of it turned
thing like it – it's a likeness   over – not shaped like back
of a flower – attempt to por-   of picture but colors like
tray a likeness of something.   this, green leaves – but this
                                  is more nearly a likeness of
                                  some South American
                                  exotic flower. Similar to
                                  the Bird of Paradise flower
                                  but much more unique to
                                  my knowledge.
                                  W CF- P1

TAT

1.   Well, this is a boy meditating over a violin and his music.
Probably in the middle of a lesson, practicing for a lesson, and
he's probably got good thoughts and bad thoughts about it. He
wishes he could play and not practice. Yet, this violin is mystic

and beautiful to him, and he wishes he could play it like his teacher does. Can't tell, might be a boy with bad eyesight. Can't tell if that's so, but it might well be — eyelids come down. Might very well be that he can't play like other children play, but yet he gets as much fun out of it as they do. Could go on filling in details, but that's essentially what that picture means to me.

2.   This is the sort of picture that depicts the history of the state or history of the people. Essentially agrarian or farm type, people close to the soil, hard working, thrifty, and with an eye toward history, and also an eye toward the future with high standards. The far-away look in the two women's eyes indicates the dream of the future that's always better than the past, yet a respect for the past. That's a good picture, the kind of picture that might be used for a state seal. A lot of spiritual stability in those people.

3 BM. Well, this is a picture of despair. Can hardly tell whether it's a man or a woman. Can hardly tell whether it's a razor or a gun beside the person. This person is in trouble. This person — I think we'll call it a woman — she placed her ideals in life in the wrong place and they have let her down and she's filled with despair. She may even have thoughts of doing away with herself, and she needs a kind, gentle, loving hand.

4.   Well, here is a husband and wife, and the wife is doing her best to get the husband to change his mind about something. There is more or less a lustful looking picture, temptress looking woman in the background. The man is a loving man toward his wife, but he's got a big decision about getting away from a bad environment or some part of it. This to me looks like she's gonna succeed.

8 BM.   This is a picture of a young man, envisioning himself as a surgeon and yet having present with him a rifle which has probably been given to him by his father, or some person, as a means of killing — not for killing man — and he sees a choice of

serving man or killing animals — maybe even serving man or killing man, and the aspect of serving man is overcoming the foolishness and he's got a resolute look of his face as though the decision is already made.

7 BM.   This is a kindly, loving, understanding young man looking at a bitter young man, trying to find words to soften the young man's heart. This is a great pleasure to the older man and the young man is just barely able to hear the old man, much less to perceive what the older man means.

13 B.   This is a little fellow that is poor in worldly goods but rich spiritually. Life is happy for him. He loves where he is and he is thinking about some big adventure that he is about to undertake and he's planning it out right now, and he's just about ready to get up and start. Probably something like seeing whether the cow is really in that pen good or whether that gate is loose. Got a little fellow like that.

5.   Well, this is a difficult story here because this woman is looking in on her daughter and her boyfriend in the living room, and the hour is late but she likes this boy and she doesn't want to interrupt yet because she is a good mother and a good woman. She feels like she ought to, and she almost busted in the room, but she'll probably pull out and go away.

13 MF.   This is a picture of a typical TV show or typical dime novel show — very unrealistic and a product of a bad mind. Kinda thing that's doing tremendous damage to our country.

6 BM.   This man has just told his mother that he's going to get married and she is startled and she hasn't decided whether she's pleased or displeased. But the son will wait only a short time and then leave, but the son has firmly made his mind up — so firmly that he won't even put his hat down. He's young and thoughtless of his mother, but a good boy, nevertheless.

16.   Well, this is the story of a lot of children who are playing with sleds and slides on a hillside. There's a fresh snow on the ground and on the trees, and the children are riding down the side of a hill and sliding down, and two men are pulling their children up the hill on sleds and nobody is cold yet because it's just started and everyone is having a wonderful time.

18 GF.   ...Well, this is...a tragedy...a housewife is...is...found a man at the bottom of a stairway. She doesn't know whether he's dead or not; suppose he's not dead because he's too far up off the floor. She doesn't know what to do about it. She's a woman of good sense because she's not screaming and hollering. She's not surprised, but she's emotionally very upset. She's making up her mind by looking at this man what she should do and she has about decided that it won't make any difference. This is not her husband but someone she thinks a good bit of. (Difference) That he's near death, that is, but don't think you need to put that in to make a good story — or if not near death, doctor couldn't help him — maybe drunk.

CHAPTER VIII

Mr. P: A System of Warding Off Confusion

The next case broadens the perspective of adaptive systems that can develop in the absence of the synthetic function. As we view this man, efforts to maintain ego functioning, reality contact, and personal integrity do not proceed via constriction as in the case of Mr. B, nor do they depend entirely upon environmental help, as in Mrs. K. This man's efforts are directive and have some system, but unlike Mr. D, he is able to persevere, cling to his pattern, and achieve some stability. As in the other cases, our appraisal of faulty ego ·functioning is reached through an analysis of what this man appears to be struggling to defend against, as well as specific defects. We see the basic problem as centering on the maintenance of some form of ego organization.

A military officer had applied for psychiatric help for his 16-year-old son. As part of a complete clinical evaluation the parents were interviewed and tested. The father expressed a desire to cooperate as an accommodation in the procedure. He held a very responsible position in the service; his record was unblemished by any indication of personality disturbance. He was in direct line for promotion to a position of much greater responsibility. The protocols of the psychological examination begin on page 158.

EFFORTS TO CONTROL

This man's first line of adaptive orientation appears to be to keep control within his own hands. Needless to say, the psychological examination is not conducive to this style and the examiner does not succumb to the patient's efforts to shift the focus to a peer relationship centered on the patient's interests, achievements, and personal reminiscences. Efforts to control also emerge in a secondary stratagem as the patient attempts to force derogatory definitions on the material he faces: something that looks hideous but "doesn't scare" him, something that really makes no sense, "belongs together because it's practically worthless," "depends on semantics." We observe this man's more desperate efforts in sharper focus when he falters in his ability to meaningfully encompass the data or tasks that face him. At these points, this man demonstrates a hyper-vigilance, a suspicion, and a search for clues that he can utilize. Constriction or withdrawal are not his modes. He must keep all data and phenomena within an organized system under his control. One form of this is to view threatened difficulty as not difficult and the external as inadequate in some way.

WHAT IS GUARDED AGAINST

The danger that this man faces is more than the discomfort of feeling inadequate. Several aspects reflect a pattern of ego-defect in the areas of part process fusion (arbitrary or random relationship), loss of distance and loss of separateness from outer reality, and lack of emotional relevance and depth. Part process fusion is best illustrated in the BRL Sorting Test where we find that this man has developed arbitrary categories delineated along the lines of his individual past experience rather than conceptual properties intrinsic to the test materials. In such instances perception does not function autonomously; reality testing functions are not carried out to determine the adequacy of perceptual products in relationship to reality demand, and concepts from sources unrelated to the reality demands intrude into the conceptual process.

This point of arbitrary part process fusion is not easily separated from the correlated element of loss of perspective between mental events that originate within the patient and what exists in outer reality. This man has lost "distance" or perspective on his relationship to external phenomena when he imbues such phenomena with intention. For example, on Rorschach Card II he says, "I don't know what it's doing — must be playing tricks"; on Rorschach Card X, "Silly looking rascals...just fantasy. . .look at one another ferociously — I don't think anyone will get hurt." It is one thing to recognize the Rorschach blots as liable to interpretation as organized thematic percepts; it is another to deal with one's percepts as this man does, as if their contents exist independently of one's perceptual processes.

These aspects of loss of part process distinctiveness and loss of distance from outer reality are events that occur in relationship to the weakening of organizational control. As the processes that maintain such control weaken, the basis of introspective surveillance dissolves. In his condition of confused ego processes this man loses awareness of sources, causes, effects, or in other words, as he loses the capacity to organize these mental events, he loses ability to experience them holistically. He experiences his percepts as originating outside of himself. He reacts to his creations with paranoid alarm. This point helps in appreciating this man's effort to maintain a hyperalertness. We note his special efforts to sort out fantasy and reality (in the Rorschach), to distinguish categories of real and unreal (in the Sorting Test), to emphasize the value of unambiguous rules (in his Wechsler answers), and we also note his suspicious sensitivity to the examiner's evaluation of what he produces.

As with the last two patients, a serious concern is that under test conditions we observe a phenomenon of progressive disorganization. Although this patient is capable of maintaining a degree of organization so that we never observe complete collapse of functions or complete break with reality as with Mrs. K and Mr. D, the impeding nature of such events permits us to glimpse still another set of mental phenomena. The guarded, paranoid quality contains hints of private, non-integrated ideation which is more apparent as the ego has moments of impending disorganization. Just as weakening organization undermines the patient's ability to maintain distinctions among ego functions and between self and non-self, so this weakening also erodes this man's capacity to keep a continuity of organization over time. Inner ideation is critical in such a personality because it serves the function of providing an ongoing core of meaning in lieu of reality. Generally, these areas are discrete — private "reality" and environmental reality — but occasionally there is a difficult and awkward balance between these two forces. It is true that currently we do not see a complete break in organization, but we do sense increasing panic as this man feels the danger of confusing inner and outer "worlds" that cannot be integrated.

THE ADAPTIVE VALUE OF A PARANOID STYLE

While we have delineated some basic problems of personality structure, justice has not been done to the patient's adaptive system. There is more here than mere stubborn efforts to maintain a control system. Unlike our other case illustrations, the element of personal locus or anchorage point of experience does not appear in such great jeopardy. This may seem strange since our theoretical premise sets forth a relationship between intactness of ego organization and the capacity to function (and experience oneself) as an integrated personality over time. Mr. P, however, repeatedly manifests some indications of inner substance as a person of consistency even if this finds expression predominantly as hyper-defensive suspiciousness of what others may be trying to do to him. However, this point may be the key that helps answer the problem. The patient may find anchorage in his suspicious outlook and the outlook may find reinforcement in the phenomena that he repeatedly experiences. That is, at many points of incipient confusion he experiences his fears and ideational concerns as related to events that he places as external to himself. He girds himself with suspicious vigilance and becomes careful and guarded. This pattern can be appreciated for its dual service: it provides a system that protects the patient from disorganization as he coyly refrains from self-revelation, and it bolsters the inner system of paranoid pseudo-reality that gives some consistency and anchorage to his experience. It is, however, a vulnerable system, dependent as it is on the patient's capacity to select and control the environmental data with which he must deal. We may note that this man's past professional life in military service probably offered a predictable system of discrete, stable rules of conduct. This context of life is far different from the conditions of a psychological examination and possibly quite different from the position of responsibility for which he was slated.

The terms "paranoid style" and "processes in lieu of synthetic function" have been used in this conceptual description of Mr. P's efforts and we have suggested the functional link that makes these efforts comprehensible in an adaptive framework. A paranoid system in a person lacking synthetic function may offer substitutes for such features as would be supplied by the synthetic function if it were present. The system achieves a measure of stability of organization where a reality-based, integrated ego system is not available to give such stability. The system achieves a modicum of linkage with reality, not via reality testing processes but by way of interrelating environmental data with prior assumptions and preconceptions. This requires intelligence and a systematic vigilance to keep the system going and to prevent it from getting out of hand. One problem of this kind of functioning was illustrated in our last case as Mr. D failed in efforts to force an arbitrary framework on his experience. He could interpret what he experienced within certain idiosyncratic preconceptions, but he could not maintain this process over a span of time and he progressively lost touch with environmental data. A "good" paranoid system must interweave processes with some deference to reality, so that it encompasses reality demands over time and also so that it does not break away and ideationally spin off to the individual's own organizational detriment. A "good" paranoid system must maintain a secondary liaison with reality and this liaison provides the prerequisite harness to foster a form of ego organization.

The attempt to bridge the gap to reality makes the paranoid system similar to that of the ego's synthetic system and merits the term "parallel system." It is parallel rather than truly synchronized to reality because the basic assumptions of the system are not derived from reality. It is, again, more of an "in lieu of" interrelationship with reality. Such a system is analogous to the cumbersome "Rube Goldberg" mechanical systems that were presented in cartoon form a few years ago. It has links to reality at the point of initial impetus and at the point of final product but, aside from inefficiency, the system calls into utilization such diverse and indirect channels of relationship that its vulnerability to breakdown is greatly multiplied.

THE QUALITY OF EXPERIENCE IN A PERSON WITH THIS SYSTEM

Although we observe that this man functions outwardly with some stability, we must ask whether his system of parallel organization permits an inner experience of solidity and integrity. The answer to this is once again derived from the assumption that what the organism phenomenally experiences can only be a reflection of ego functioning. Thus, the stream of experience is a product of the stream of mental events.

We assume that in this man mental events are not products of a synthetic function that gears inner emotions and thoughts in coordination with outer reality to produce an experience of separateness, wholeness, and individuality. Instead there is a pattern of separation — restriction of inner ideation and affect and close adherence to a pattern of rigid, controlling interaction between person and environment. We have noted this man's tendency to find greatest comfort within a framework of rigidly prescribed (and predictable) rules of conduct. Emotional components are relatively absent. The patient's metaphor is predominantly that of machines, mechanisms, and instruments of action. His style is that of role implementation and self-identity definition via activity. Thus, in his typical mode of functioning — sterile and mechanical — we assume a corresponding state of phenomenal experience: sterile and mechanical, alleviated by fantasies that must also follow rigid mechanical requirements.

A supplementary element of this patient's experience occurs when his "in lieu of" organization falters. At these moments we postulate that experience, again, is a mirroring of mental events that occur at that moment. But at these points he loses stability of experience as he loses his control of internal events; the sharp isolation of internal and external breaks down and he loses distance from reality. At these points he experiences the panic of loss of stability and loss of identity.

All of this man's sense of worth is tied to maintaining the peculiar pattern of meaning and relationship to reality manifested. He experiences and he exists within this framework, which is inadequate by synthetic function standards but relatively stable and adaptive by schizophrenic standards. He functions, within limitations, with such adequacy that on his own he never came to the attention of authorities as mentally disturbed. The psychological test battery, however, as an environmental condition that is not easily brought within the framework of his adaptive capacity challenges that capacity as the routine stream of regimented military life does not.

TEST PROTOCOLS OF MR. P.

Wechsler-Bellevue I

	R.S.	Wt. S.
Inf.	18	13
Com.	18	16
Dig.	14	12
Arith.	11	15
Sim.	17	14
Verb.		70
P.A.	9	8
P.C.	12	12
Blks.	22	10
Obj.	18	10
Dig. S.	45	11
Perf.		51
Total	121	

Verbal IQ	128
Perf. IQ	113
Full Sc. IQ	123

Recall: Imm.   19
         Delay   14-16

Information

1.	Before – Harry S. Truman.	1
2.	Therm – Instrument for temperature readings.	1
3.	Rubber – Tree.	1
4.	London – England, Great Britain.	1
5.	Pints – Two.	1
6.	Weeks – 52.	1
7.	Italy – Rome.	1
8.	Heart – Pumps blood through body.	1
9.	Brazil – In South America, Southeast section.	1
10.	Japan – Tokyo.	1
11.	Plane – Wright Bros.	1
12.	Tall – 5 ′ 3½ ″ or 4 ″.	1
13.	Paris – (Thinks) I've flown from here to England, 2800 miles.	1
14.	Hamlt – Shakespeare.	1
15.	Popn – 167 million.	1
16.	Wash – February, Washington, Lincoln – February – February 12.	0
17.	Pole – Most common thing – I don't know – should know – Byrd - but some Norwegian.	0

18.	Egyp – Any time limit – in Africa, northeast, along Suez.	1
19.	Finn – Mark Twain.	1
20.	Vati – Part of Rome – section of Rome – where the Pope lives – city within a city.	1
21.	Kora – Koran?, I don't know much about it.	0
22.	Faust – I don't know.	0
23.	Corp – Legal term – without due process of law – a law defending one of our basic judicial rights.	0
24.	Ethn – don't know – I'm curious.	0
25.	Apoc – I don't know.	0

Score   18

Comprehension

1.	Env – Ready to put in mailbox.	2
2.	Thea – Try to keep order. I wouldn't say anthing. I'd walk quietly to the rear, tell manager and let him take care of it. If small, put it out. If people get excited, bring order, open doors. Mob hysteria terrible.	2
3.	B. C. – Primarily because I wouldn't enjoy such company, just like propaganda, like Russians did. If you say things often enough you get to believe it, so why subject yourself to it, or if you hear something said by mouth or . . .	2
4.	Tax – To support government in many endeavors – roads, schools, hospitals. Somebody has to pay for them.	2
5.	Shoe – Well, of course, many people don't use leather for shoes. If I had my choice I'd use leather. Long wearing, durable, attractive, warm, impervious to most things if properly constructed. Some day will find something better.	2
6.	Land – many reasons – proximity or span of control if own a business. Basically, supply and demand, if many want it, price up. Taxes are higher.	2
7.	For – I should have some idea of where I was so I'd know how streams ran. I'd have a watch on. With watch and sun fix direction. Lot of variables to that one. (Talks about situations in flying) – I wouldn't panic like others because of training as a kid – better prepared than most to answer it. North side of tree has moss on it.	2
8.	Law – In any society need common rules of conduct and behavior. What is expected – no utopia. We're not civilized enough. Without laws we'd have chaos. Minority take over.	

	Not severity, but certainty of punishment, that's important. With justice certainly. Every society has laws.	2
9.	Mar — Adds something to ceremony. Important in marriage ceremony. License shows honest intent along with many other things.	0
10.	Deaf — I think I know. Obvious that you learn by example. Sight — important — primary means of learning. I don't know how you would learn to talk unless you could hear. If you make a correct sound, then instructor could give you a signal — but inflections, etc. — different — fairly obvious to me.	2

Score   18

Arithmetic

1.	4 + 5 — $9.	1
2.	6c - 10 — 4c.	1
3.	8c - 25 — 17c.	1
4.	or 36, or 4 — 9.	1
5.	2 hrs 24 mi, 3 mph — 8.	1
6.	7, 2c-50 — 36.	1
7.	7 lb, 25, $1? — 28.	1
8.	2/3 new, 400 — 600.	1
9.	42″3 yds — 9 (Read it again. Works it aloud.)	1
10.	25″96 — I guess, Doc.	2

Score   11

Similarities

1.	Or-Ba — Fruit.	2
2.	Ct-Dr — Items of Clothing.	2
3.	Dg-Ln — Animals.	2
4.	Wn-Bi — Toys.	1
5.	Pa-Ra — Communication.	2
6.	Ar-Wr — Matter.	0
7.	Wo-Al — Flammable — will burn.	1
8.	Ey-Er — Senses — are instruments of the body that give us two of our senses.	2
9.	Eg-Sd — Start of life or could be — if — in proper environment could be considered the start of life.	2
10.	Po-St — Evidences of culture.	1
11.	Pr-Pu — Means of guiding behavior — two of several.	2

12.   Fl-Tr – One word, Doc – I don't know – it would take me
      ten minutes.   0
                                                    Score   ⎯⎯
                                                             17

Picture Completion

1.   Gl – Bridge of lady's nose.   1
2.   Mn – Left side of gentleman's mustache.   1
3.   Mn – This gentleman's ear.   1
4.   Cd – Not missing. The 9 or the 6 is upside down, one or
     the other.   0
5.   Cr – One of the claws on the crayfish or lobster.   1
6.   Pg – Tail.   1
7.   Bt – Stock.   1
8.   Dr – Door knob.   1
9.   Wch – Second hand.   1
10. Pchr – Should be some water. (I have to ask him to explain
     where.)   1
11. Mr – Leg (?) Chair. Should be able to see all four legs, but
     I don't know how detailed it is supposed to be.   0
12. Mn – Tie – but that's debatable. I don't know where he's
     going.   1
13. Blb – An incandescent job, got a filament. Threads for
     connection – piece of lead down here.   1
14. Gl – You wouldn't want me to say shoulders. I don't see
     anybody. All lower detail missing – her hips, thighs, calves,
     but shoes.   0
15. Sh – Shadow behind the man.   1
                                                    Score   ⎯⎯
                                                             12

Digit Span

Digits Forward 7   Digits Backward 7   Score   14

Picture Arrangement

Hse	4″	ok	2	Man building a house – laid foundation – processed lumber – erected the scaffolding – structure – completes it – painting it.
Hold	18″	ok	2	Robber – armed robber – holding up gentleman – taking his wallet – caught – judge and jury – sentenced to prison where he remains.

Elev	23"	ok	2	Looking down an elevator – hears the ring – rising – doors pushed open – see two people – all three up – come to rest – one leaving it – warehouse equipment elevator.
Flirt	60" 68"	JANET JNAET	3	King – chauffeur – big car – going along at good pace – spots lady with burden – orders chauffeur to stop which he does – king dismounts – says something gallant to the lady – carries her burden – car, I don't know where it's going – chauffeur thinks king has lost his marbles.
Fish	10"	GH EI	0	(Studies carefully – can't seem to get idea – won't be rushed) – I don't know what kind of story to make out of this one. (Makes up story of them as they are.) (I suggest rearranging them.) Well, well, It's his frustration – he wanted to get a little relaxation and fish – had bait – lost one and bait – then caught a couple – found out some character in diving suit stole his fish – walked off in a huff – stupid story – no doubt the wrong one.
		Score	9	

BRL Sorting Test

PART I

STIMULUS OBJECT	SORT AND VERBALIZATION	SCORE
Sugar cube (Free choice)	Spoon, other sugar cube. (Story about riding horse this morning) Well I guess the spoon, but he	

	(horse) doesn't use spoon and I don't use cube sugar – well, in restaurant use spoon. Well in restaurant, see sugar, use spoon to get it.	Fab
Pipe	<u>Cigar, cigarette, rubber cigar.</u> Have to come out and see my horse – how do you mean goes with it – belongs with it? If had no tobacco – cigar goes with it. Nothing, but if you have no tobacco. Just cigarette and cigar. I'd give that to my dog.	Fab
Toy pliers	<u>Real tools, toy tools.</u> Are you assuming this is usable – well, might as well have other toys. And these daddy can use – all tools – some toy and some real. These are as good as I have at home. These for little kiddies to tear up furniture with.	CD S/N
Ball	I don't know what this is – sink stopper – could get a conditioned response with this (bell) and salivation with your pooch. Normally I would say nothing belongs with the ball.	Fail
Fork	<u>Real silverware.</u> This is business for eating – i.e., you're not playing so I wouldn't put the toy ones with it – normal utensils when you eat.	FD n
Paper disc	<u>Paper, file card, matches</u> (took matches away). This worthless to me and I wouldn't put anything with it (?) Well, as worthless to me. Belong together because prac-	

	tically worthless. In Air Force we get to be packrats.	Syn
Bell	Real screwdriver. I took you too literally. Nothing. Normally don't belong together, but depends on what you want to do.	Fail

PART II

SORT	VERBALIZATION	SCORE
Smoking	Similar because of smoking or habit of smoking — matches once used for it.	CD →C
Metal	Well, all metal. Similar in that respect. Don't necessarily belong together. Probably would not normally be together. Eating vs. utility — bell — mechanical — pliers — mechanical and I guess eating could be mechanical.	CD CD→Syn
Round	I don't know, Doc. They are things — all depends on semantics. I could make up a story about it. Am I not cooperating?	Fail
Tools	These two useful — I could take these two if given to me and give it to kids but I don't know about boys. This could be in a store (toys) but — as an incentive give dad these cheap but usable toys.	Fab
Paper	Because practically worthless. I guess you want to see what's in my mind. (Smiles secretively)	Syn
Doubles	Don't belong together — wouldn't normally be together — only reason — you put them to see what I would say. Put these in individual groups —	

	toy with utility (breaks it up into useful toy vs. identities). I thought I had to consider everything vs. everything else. (Q) Two of each.	Arbitrary → CD
Red	All red — and same shade.	CD
Silverware	All metal — and are similar even though half toys — well, you get the thought of eating. You don't want me to tell you the obvious.	(CD)
Rubber	Rubber. (suspicious glance)	CD
White	All white.	CD
Toys	Items of play, enjoyment, recreation — all toys — novelties.	CD
Rectangles	My youngest daughter would enjoy them. One reason — if I have to give a reason — sugar reminds me here of horse — like colors. (Tries to pull nail out of block.)	Fab

Rorschach Protocol

FREE RESPONDING	INQUIRY

I.   10″   1. Looks like you took a piece of paper, put ink on it and folded it. It's symmetrical and real fast — one-tenth of a second — could be construed as a bat — in flight - well no (waves card around, sets it down).
2. If you look closely it looks like a woman's torso — calves — large — toe sticking out — knee — above that — vague — might have on large

1.Bat — in flight
W FM+ A P
2. Hips — well formed — just from the waist down — legs close together. (D3)
Large hat — breast area.
D3 → dr M+ Hd
          M-
3. (Large D1 area.)
Two heads — all that junk — they usually put on them.
dr F - Hd

hat – looking away from
you.
3. Sort of a hideous looking
thing up here. Sort of
scary – not to be – but could
be used that way.

Add: I've seen Valley
Forge – chasing out with
cape – gun (D8) – moving
fast – and what it is in between the two gentlemen, I
don't know.
DW   M- H

2½′

II.   10″   1. Well, two poodles –
shoulders up – noses up –
standing up – facing one
another like so. I don't know
what is in the middle –
balancing something. The red
stuff I don't know what that
is – above their heads, below
their paws and above their
eyes.
(Wants to set it down.)
That's about all.
Oh, you could see something
here, but my imagination is
not too good. I don't know
what it's doing – must be
playing tricks. (Can't figure
out what D4 is.) If someone
were to say what is that or
I'll kill you, I would say two
1½′   poodles.

1. I don't know. Front
shoulder joint – in here.
(Goes on and on about
proportions.)
W   FM+   A P

III.   10″   1. This gives the indication of
people here – these two –
God, odd looking types – could
be construed that they are
dressed formally – men with
arms down – doing something
– may be their stuffed shirts –
bulging out – of course, could
be a night club shot – dress
shirt – black – and red – oh,
seems out of place. Of course,

1. Idiots – hurrying and
scurrying – odd looking –
fowl-like, in formal attire.
Shoes – high heeled – that
doesn't add up – maybe a
shadow. Head looks like a
chicken's – grotesque –
don't look like human –
two characters in an act.
D8   M   (H) (P)
(Contam.)

the whole thing doesn't make
too much sense. Two turkey-
1'50" ish-looking men – fowl-like.

IV.   10"   1. Looks like a skin of an   1. Fur – looks furry.
              animal flattened out. I   W Fc+A, obj   P
              wouldn't attempt to say what
              kind with that head – eyes –
              protrudence of eyes – fangs –
              but does look like a backbone
              here and tail.
              Don't look like much of any-
       70"   thing, Doc, between you and me.

V.   (Looks at back of card.)   1. Mostly wings – small
       20   1. Doesn't remind me of any-   body – little head – feet
              thing I've ever seen. Most of   out here. I don't know
              them look like bats so far –   what these are (head pro-
              these five –   jections). Do bats have
       40   except those men.   these?
              Nothing, well generally a bat.   W F+ A P
              If saw it rapidly – a bat –
       1'15" but to study it, no.

VI.   (Whistles through teeth.)
       35"   Same as last one.
       45"   1. There's a suggestion of a   1. (Cutting out D2) Hide
              skin – of course, there's a   with fur out.
              suggestion of a backbone,   W Fc+ A, obj. P
              but damn poor taxidermy —
              so damn much stuff hanging
              down.
              Legs – shade of fur – but
       1'40" from here on up – no.

VII.   35"   Can't see it – reminds me of   Add: W KF   Clds
              nothing. Wouldn't be clouds –   (Denied)
              they aren't shaped that way.
              I'd like to say something but
              I just can't see it.

VIII.   (Able to pick up subtleties of
              E's reactions.)

50″ 1. Fairly good three-quarter shot from the rear of an animal – the head of an animal – like a bear – most of weight on hind leg – like pushing off – odd color for bear – I guess on snow and sun going down might get that
2′10″ pinkish tint to it.
But as to rest of blob, reminds me of nothing – reads back of card.

1. Most of weight on right rear – stepping over – ear – eye – bear nose – right hind leg looks to be normal – well formed – right front – abnormal – hind leg too long.
D FM+, FC A P

IX. 25 1. All look sort of hideous in a way. They are trying to put out something to me – but I don't like them. They're trying to tell you there's a skull there and some horns like a horror movie – not trying to frighten me, I'm sure. Very poor skull – eyes elongated the wrong way – all in color – that way as if they want you to see a skull
2″ or some horns or some damn thing.

1. Over all – nothing. If they want me to see something – could be a skull – like out between this stuff, whatever that is.
D   S F- At

X. 45″ That doesn't make sense. Doc, there's nothing there.
1. Silly looking rascals – look at one another – mouths open – got eyes but certainly phantasy – nothing on earth – just phantasy.
2. Dragons here or a horse.
3. Looks like a young colt's
1′25″ head here – only the head.

1. Like funny men from some other world - mouth - funny eyes – odd looking – funny things on top of head – look at one another ferociously – I don't think anyone will get hurt.
D4 M   (H)
2. Whole thing – a great big stupid dragon with many things on it – but then – a colt.
D$_1$ F-   (A)

3. (D$_1$) – colt's head –
eye – behind something. I
love animals.
D$_1$ F- Ad

TAT

1. This looks like a boy with a burning desire to be a concert violinist. He is daydreaming about what he would like to be and what he thinks he can be, because he looks like he is intelligent and stable. He is dreaming about his future. He wants to be the world's best, and I would predict that he would be a good violinist. I don't think you would find any juvenile delinquency in that pose.

18 BM. This gentleman appears to be sort of drunk. He has the stomach of a drunk, inherently thin, but has a paunch, and he is either being restrained or forceably ejected from some place. He's got his overcoat on, and you'll find a lot of places where drunks will frequent and won't remove their overcoats – just sit and have three or four quick shots.

4. This is a man and wife and she is obviously trying to convince him that what he is going to do (and I don't know what) is wrong, and she's restraining him and he is determined to do it. Very short story.

17 BM. I guess this is a circus performer, the way he is built. He's climbing up to do his act. His hair is too long for a circus performer.

7 BM. Looks like a lawyer and his client in court. The lawyer is the elderly gentleman. The young gentleman is listening to a person on the witness chair, not too happily.

12 M. Stories – humph – looks like hypnosis, Doc. Enough.

11.   Well, these animals and people are going over a gorge or a bridge. It must be horrible weather to their rear. Forward looks like good weather, but then you see this big cliff with no way out except to the left. The road goes down to the sun. Looks like it is in the Andes, the Aztecs with their big llamas. They make good blankets.

10.   This is a man and wife embracing — moment of tenderness. There could be a lot of stories.

13 B.   Well, I see the ax marks on the old log cabin. It was built by hand. The door is out of kilter. The little boy looks healthy but poor. He's just there — just a poor boy. It's a summer day. He's sitting in the sun and just thinking about squirrels.

12 F.   Well, this is Evil in the rear whispering to the virtuous one trying to get the virtuous one to do wrong. By the leer on the face of the evil one I think she is successful, by the look of pleasant anticipation.

9 BM.   (Takes card himself. "What time, Doc?") They are tired. As you know, they have been working for days and long hours. They are catching a few winks.

14.   This is a young boy. It's early. He doesn't want to awaken his family. He looks out the window. He has his brother in the room and doesn't want to turn the light on. If it's in the fall, he's looking for ducks.

13 MF.   Well, this man has had intercourse and he's ashamed of himself, and I guess the young lady has passed out. (?) Well, circumstances show this is not a marriage scene. She wouldn't be draped like that, would have on a nightgown or pajamas. The whole thing — maybe I am of a suspicious nature. Single bed.

15.   I wouldn't know why he's in the graveyard other than to pay his respects. He's an old man, lonesome, and this is one of his loved ones. He went to say his prayers.

A Supplementary Manual for the Sorting Test

A thorough discussion of concept formation and its relationship to thought processes and ego organization is to be found in Volume I of Rapaport's *Diagnostic Psychological Testing* or Holt's recent revision of this book. The following constitutes a supplement and contains amplification, finer discriminations, and implications for understanding ego functioning which the authors have found useful. We have given enough elaboration so that the manual can stand as a guide for usage, but familiarity with Rapaport's concepts will provide a broader background.[1]

ADMINISTRATION

The test material consists of 33 common objects from which the subject must select groupings to make meaningful conceptual and communicable sortings. The items are listed on page 191. In the part administered first, Part I, the patient is asked to sort or generate his conceptual patterns in response to starter items that are offered him. Part II, administered later, asks the patient to recognize and describe the patterns implicit in the clusters made by the examiner. This requires a more acquiescent "passive" stance on the part of the patient in contrast to the requirement for a more "active" approach in Part I. That is, in Part II the patient is required merely to recognize "structure" as it is given; in Part I, he has to engage in creative, selective, and judgmental functions

---

[1] A quantitative scoring system for the Scoring Test developed by Colarelli and Siegel (1966) should also prove useful to practitioners who discover the utility of this test.

since choices are open to him as to how to "take off" from the stimulus object and how to end up with a satisfactory product.

The patient is seated comfortably across a work space from the examiner, who takes the test objects, a few at a time, out of a box and sets them randomly in one area. The patient is asked, *"Is there anything here that you don't recognize?"* (or "Is there anything you don't know?"). If the patient queries about one or more objects, the examiner asks him what he thinks each item might be and agrees if the patient is correct. The patient generally knows what the items are but is surprised at their "ordinariness" and may want to know if there might be some hidden or subtle meanings that he is not catching. If needed, the examiner offers a minimal correct description (e.g., "That is a piece of paper.").

On beginning Part I, E says, *"Now look these things over and quickly choose one and put it here."* This is item 1 of Part I where the patient chooses his own starting object. As soon as the patient has made his choice, E says, *"Now put everything that you think belongs with it over here and let me know when you are done."* When the patient accomplishes this, E says, *"Now tell me why these things belong together."* The patient's starting item, his sorting (including sequence of choices), and all of his verbal comments are noted. E also notes any spatial pattern of object placement. E then places the objects that have been used back with the others and goes on to the next item. In the remainder of Part I, E does the placing of each starter item and says, *"Now put everything that you think belongs with this over here with it."*[2] When this is done he again asks the patient to state the reason for belongingness: *"Now tell me why they belong together."*

If a patient refuses to make a sort or says that he can't see ". . .anything that would go with that," E encourages first by waiting expectantly for the patient to comply and later by

[2]The sequence of starter items is: 2. Fork, 3. Pipe, 4. Bell, 5. Paper disc, 6. Toy pliers, 7. Ball.

repeating the instruction, *"Put everything that belongs. . ."* or *"Take your time."*

To begin Part II, E says, *"Now I'm going to put these out here and I want you to tell me why they belong together."* E then places the first cluster for Part II and asks *"Why do they belong together?"* After the patient responds, E places the items back in the main area and makes his second placement, repeating the process. For the sake of standard procedure, we place all items back in the main area before going on to a new sort even when some of the items from the last sorting will be included in the next placement. (See page 190 for listing of sequence of groupings in Part II.)

The patient will occasionally not attempt to give an explanation of why the items have been placed together. Sometimes, of course, this is because he has no organized concept clearly in mind. Frequently, it is because he is afraid that the concept that comes to his mind may be considered inadequate by the examiner. However, the examiner should encourage the patient to give this material, making note that it came with more prodding. One way of prodding is to say, *"Take your time,"* implying that the examiner is unwilling to settle for a default and will wait out the patient. By obtaining these "intermediate" responses, the examiner can gain more data regarding the patient's functioning. He is better able to assess what kinds of pathological functioning take place and produce certain thinking; he is also better able to gauge how self-screening operates to help overcome this kind of pathology. Both kinds of data are important: the pathological trends *and* the "adaptive" or suppressive functions that indicate some intact ego screening functions.

After Part II has been completed, E may go back to items where the patient could give no response and determine whether the patient can pick out the response that "fits" if he is offered a range of possibilities. E may say, *"Could it be size, shape, color, use?"* The patient's ability (or inability) to determine the appropriate concept with this added information (or structure) constitutes additional data in determining degree of ego weakness. The level of support needed to permit the patient to recognize and select "appropriateness" in the test is an indication of how adequately the ego will function in non-test situations and what degree of support may be needed in such situations to achieve adequate functioning.

It is also important to note additions or shifts in the patient's responses. On both parts of the test, the examiner should communicate his openness to "after-thoughts." Sometimes, in the course of his sorting or describing the sort, or as he waits for E to finish writing, the patient "realizes" an alternative response and grasps that it is "better." This certainly connotes some capacity for self-reflection or evaluation and judgment, and constitutes important data bearing on ego functioning. Similarly, if the patient "spoils" a response, or after an adequate response offers further but irrelevant or tangential associations that carry him away from his first approximation, these data are revealing of ego functioning. These behaviors are indicative of the effectiveness of self-regulating or self-screening functions or what might be referred to as self-generated "feedback." Where a response is given and later the patient appears to recognize its inadequacies, he apparently detected something wrong but was not functioning effectively enough to immediately screen the response or locate the flaw. The fact that some recognition of inadequacy did not take place describes the possibility that ego screening and ego judgment are temporarily overwhelmed rather than destroyed and that with some "orientation" or reality structuring, this kind of functioning can be re-established.

SCORING

The basic rationale for scoring in terms of a framework of ego or thought organization is contained in Rapaport's chapter cited above. Part I of the test is scored in terms of *Conceptual Level* and *Conceptual Span.* In Part II only *Conceptual Level* is scored.[3]

Conceptual Level refers to the level of conceptualization selected by the patient in giving the cluster of objects being considered an appropriately meaningful designation. Thus, the description of the smoking items as, "Things my Dad would use to relax after dinner," concretizes the concept beyond what the data of the objects themselves afford.

The scoring of conceptual level is really an estimate of the manner in which the patient can locate and use conceptual dimensions intrinsic to the population of objects with which he is dealing. In this sense conceptual level is close to a coding for behavior quite similar to the F+% in the Rorschach. It is an ego strength measure in the broad sense of determining how effectively several ego functions are working in interaction: perception of the demands of the task, emergence of responsive associations that can be screened, channeled, and integrated, and judgment about how to communicate the response.

Concept Span refers to the manner in which the patient has implemented his conceptual level. That is, once he has a concept that he is using as a basis of discriminating "belonging" from "non-belonging," how discerning and consistent is he about appropriate inclusion and exclusion? Thus, concept span is an extension of conceptual level and indicates consistency of usage. In this way it also contributes as a measure of "ego strength."

[3] One exception occurs when a "split narrow" scoring can be made to a Part II response. See Rapaport.

A. *Conceptual Level Scoring*

The scoring categories of Conceptual, Functional, Concrete, and Failure are the basic categories described by Rapaport and will be briefly described here.

Conceptual Definition (CD) is an optimum communication demarcating the discreteness of a group of objects from those remaining yet connoting the internal unity of the grouping. Thus, if the large and small silverware are placed to form one sorting, the level of communication that is most meaningful in terms of why these items have a discrete classification is that they are "silverware." It is, of course, not wrong to refer to them as, "things you would use to eat with" or "made out of metal," but the latter two definitions do not "zero in" on the critical identity of this cluster with the same communicative incisiveness. It is like referring to a book as, "something readable" or "that paper thing." The implication of the scoring is, however, not merely whether the "message sender" is able to gauge whether the receiver will grasp a concept congruent to his, but how a person organizes his perceptions and thoughts. To the degree that conceptual definitions are used, these are indications of effective operation of ego functions that utilize environmental data and permit the data to retain current relevant meaning rather than to be aligned with personal or idiosyncratic concepts that weaken the distinctive meaningfulness of current data.

The *Functional Definition* (FD), as the term implies, defines the grouping in terms of one facet of its properties, its functional side. Frequently, the functional and the conceptual definitions overlap in terms of their level of adequacy. For example, in the "smoking" sort of Part II, the phrase "smoking things," or "things you use for smoking," or "used to smoke with," are not very different and a CD would be merited in each case. On the other hand, in the Part II sorting of tools, there is a discrepancy between the kind of thinking reflected by the word "tool" and that reflected in "things you fix with." What may be reflected is not merely word finding difficulty or a problem in maintaining an abstract level of perception, although such problems will influence concept level, but the way in which a patient works at the problem of organizing his perception, how he understands what constitutes a "consensual" level of organization, and how he communicates his understanding. The word "consensual" is critical here. It implies complex ego functioning in the nature of relating inner conceptual associations to the "assumed" or "understood" criteria of external reality. In a sense the patient is always asking himself something like this: "The cluster of items can have meaning to me in a number of ways and some of these I know are idiosyncratic to me. But what demarcations can be used that might constitute a perception shared by a number of other persons? Where would our conceptual thinking overlap? Is this what I should say as an answer?" Thus, the conceptual level that emerges tends to reflect the person's conceptual grasp or, said another way, his style of perceptual organization modified by his awareness of reality considerations involved in communication.

The *Concrete Definition* (C) refers to a categorization that captures either partial qualities of the items or is over-inclusive along some restricted and concrete dimensions. That is, the concept refers to object properties which are close to the data of sensory impression or fall short of communicating the sorting in terms of a completed perceptual act. Thus, the "silverware" referred to as "metal" connotes that the patient has not moved beyond recognizing one facet of the data available to him (its material constituents).

A useful distinction between the functional and concrete response is that functional implies that the patient at some level recognizes the conceptual level category but is not able to discriminatingly select it as his verbal response; the concrete level implies that the patient is unable to move from a perception of some of the properties of the objects to a recognition of the essential property separating the objects from those which are not included.

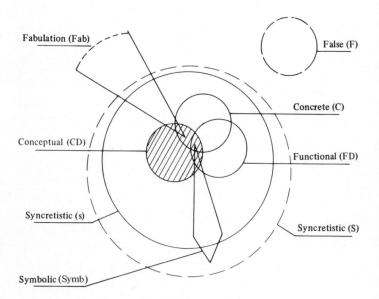

Fig. 3. Schematic Representation Showing Relationships among Sorting Test Scoring Categories.

Figure 3 presents a schematic representation of the relationship among the scoring categories. The CD (Conceptual Definition) scoring forms an anchor or reference point in this representation. A FD (Functional Definition) captures some properties of this classification yet it is co-extensive with material which exists beyond the intrinsic limits of the grouping, i.e., other items can share the same function. AC (Concrete) category similarly has the potential for reference to 'objects farther beyond the grouping itself. A False (F) or incorrect response misses the target and is represented as isolated from areas covered by the other response categories.

The following are categories that need to be added or amplified because of their specific value in yielding further information regarding patterns of ego functioning.

False CD: (-CD). It sometimes happens that a patient gives a verbalization which is on a good conceptual level but which is simply inappropriate for the grouping. For example, "They are all toys," is a CD, but when it is given to a paper sorting, it is obviously inadequate. Formerly such definitions were given the score, *False.* It is more meaningful to preserve the level of conceptualization on which the patient makes his attempt even though it is false; therefore in the example given, the scoring would be, False CD (-CD). The scoring points out while some ego functions are likely to be intact (e.g., recognizing some conceptual categories relevant to the kinds of objects being used), the fact that this ability cannot be anchored or used effectively is ominous. The connotation is that there is some impairment in the capacity for reviewing and screening ideas, testing their suitability, and gaining a perspective on one's own appropriateness.

Syncretistic: (s and S). A syncretistic response places the grouping of objects within such broad parameters that the classification loses specific distinction. There, however, is one kind of frequently found syncretistic response which has less serious pathological implications. This is the syncretistic response based on location or source, as for example: "They're all objects found in a drawer," "around the house," "all man-made." These responses indicate rather weak and inadequate strainings for concepts and though they do imply a certain amount of organizational loosening, they do not have the same implications as syncretic responses which imply more devious or contrived inclusions as "All nonconductors of electricity," or "all could be used to injure."

This latter type of response is more indicative of the phenomenon of "loosening of associations." An association of many possible associations is arbitrarily embraced as the idea to be used conceptually. One can see that moving from one such arbitrarily fixed association to the next without evidence of self-scrutiny or efforts at locating one's point of departure allows thought to wander and organization to be lost. The former, less pathological, type of syncretistic response is coded with a small script s; the latter with a capital S. In the schematic diagram, the very large area is labeled "S" for syncretistic, implying the potential for broad over-inclusiveness of the conceptual approach.

Fabulations (Fab) and *Symbolic* Responses (Symb). A distinction must be made between responses that include strained interpretative ideas that conceivably could be correctly implied and those in which the concept is based on an idiosyncratic and arbitrary association. The former is scored as a fabulation (Fab) and the latter as a symbolization (Symb).

Fabulations include such responses as interpretation of the paper forms as schematic representations of coasters, napkins, or ash trays and so, together with silverware, they could form a "table setting." Symbolic responses would include the response to a tool sorting as "stands for manliness" or to the red objects as "means danger" or to the smoking items as "represents desire." Again, such interpretations are not intrinsically wrong; they do, however, indicate deficiencies in the guiding, screening, or tracking processes which might evaluate and control direction of thought, since such answers lack an element of appropriateness.

There are also two degrees of severity of responses in which the patient has introduced thematic ideas. When the description is gratuitous but appears to be recognized as such, it is a fabulation: "This silverware could be for a mother and then this would be for a daughter," or "The man could be smoking a cigarette and then maybe he decides to smoke a pipe or a cigar." When thematic inferences go clearly beyond the data with a loss of awareness of the tenuousness of the ideas, the scoring is symbolic: "This means that two people are eating and three people are smoking," or, "This is a meal; the sugar means coffee, the paper is a cereal box."

It should be noted that some items are linked in a setting because of their concrete uses. For example, the screwdriver is placed with the bell, and the verbalization that is given is, "You need the screwdriver to put it on with." The linkage here is via the concrete properties and is scored concrete (C) rather than fabulation.

Chain: Ch and R-Ch. There are two types of chain definitions distinguished by the symbols Ch for the serial linking of objects together without reference back to the starting point, and R-Ch for the radial chain, in which objects are related by separate and different links to a central object, but each radius remains unrelated to the others. An example of a Ch (serial) would be: with the paper disk in Part I, the patient sorts the ball because they are both round, then adds the rubber cigar because it and the ball are both rubber, and finally includes the real cigar because it is also a cigar. An example of a radial chain (R-Ch) is as follows: "I would relate them all to the bell. The ball goes with it because it is a toy, too; the disk could be the button you push to ring a door bell; the person who rings the bell might smoke the cigarette; and these (corks and sink stopper) could be used to dampen it, keep it from making too much noise." The chain scoring category is used to connote the "drifting" quality of thought organization. Although this kind of functioning may be true of severe obsessive personalities, the shifting from one concept to another also suggests an inability to define relevance or comparative adequacy against any reality-based set of experiences. In the serial form of the chain response, the connotation is loss of functional awareness of starting point and sequence; that is, impairment in those functions that guide or oversee cognitive functions.

Fabulative elements are very likely to be evident in chaining responses, as in the following example: On Part I the patient sorts to the bell and says, "This is a bell on a house. The house has lock and key; and if it is broke you need to fix it with the screwdriver. Person who fixes it smokes so they're all together (adds related items)." The return to the original object at the end is one indication that this is not a true chain and the linking of objects in a "story" indicates that the response should be considered a fabulation. It was scored "Fabulation with tendency to chain" ("Fab→Ch") because there is real chaining in the transition from tools, "to fix it," to something "for the repairman to smoke." Incidentally, in the present example, it is not clear whether the "it" that is to be fixed is the bell or the lock; if the latter was meant, there is less of a radial chain aspect and more straight "Ch" involved.

As indicated above, it is necessary to distinguish carefully between radial chains and what might be called "multiple-narrow" sortings or verbalizations, especially on Part I. Thus, an obsessive, doubt-ridden patient who cannot decide which attribute of the sample object to work with may make, either successively or simultaneously, several sortings on different bases. For example: with the ball, a patient may sort the eraser because it is rubber; he may add the corks because they are round and also the hammer because it is a toy. This really constitutes several responses or a cluster of narrow "CD's" that should be scored as such. This type of response does not have the diagnostic implications of the chain and is given by neurotics as well as by psychotics and persons with character disorders.

B. *Scoring of Concept Span.*

The span of each of the patient's sorts in Part I is scored along a dimension from "narrowness" to "looseness." Following is the seven-point scoring scale used by Rapaport:

7–POINT SCALE

N – Very Narrow		1 – Slightly Loose
	+ Appropriate	
(N) – Narrow	Adequate	(L) – Loose
n – Slightly Narrow		L – Very Loose

From one point of view, concept span describes the degree to which the patient adheres to or implements his conceptual framework. Thus, if the patient adopts a working concept of "toys" on Part I, but includes the large screwdriver along with the toy silverware, toy tools, candy cigarettes, and play cigar, we suspect some difficulty in interpretation of the properties of the objects in relationship to the stated basis of organization. This response would be scored slightly loose "(1)" or loose "(L)" depending on the mitigating influence of a possible explanation. Similarly, if the patient has created a sorting of paper items and labeled it "paper or cardboard," we could score it on the narrow side if it included the cardboard circle, square, and 3 x 5 card, but omitted the match book and cigarette. In this case the score should be narrow (N) in recognition of the fact that legitimate paper objects are omitted.

These scores help detect ego function difficulties (or reassure that these difficulties are absent) because they focus closely on the flaws in implementation of integrative and differentiating functions of the ego. We are not primarily interested in the person's capacity for conceptual thinking (although data relevant to capacity emerge) but in the ongoing refinement and guiding functions which relate thought to environmental data and oversee the synchronization of thought with such data.

Where the patient's productions are not conventional or straightforward, scoring is not easy. In these situations, however, we need to be most discerning about the fine points of scoring and their implications for the pattern of ego functioning. If in a given grouping the patient omits one or more objects that could reasonably share the sorting properties, his score is on the narrow side; if he adds what might be considered extraneous objects, his score is on the loose side. It sometimes happens that a sorting is made which bears no obvious logical relationship to the usual possibilities. If the basis for the sort is fabulated, or syncretistic, the span score will usually be "L," conveying that the properties of the objects being used are not being related to conceptual categories but derive from associated or tangential properties as the basis of organization.

There are also certain very simple or peculiar sortings which are not "adequate"; neither are they loose or narrow. For example, the bell is placed with the lock, with the explanation that, "they both go on a bicycle, " or the tools are placed with the block of wood and nail with the comment, "They are used in carpentry and here is something that is being worked on." In such cases the sorting is not loose or narrow if one recognizes the concrete premise for the organization. We note, then, that the verbalization must be considered as a context from which to evaluate span.

Considerations in scoring "Narrow." Sample scorings for various sorts are given below. When there are gross or obvious omissions, the score is "N." When the concept offered by the patient has several constraints on it, the score is "N." For example, if the sink stopper and the ball are sorted and described as "round, red, and rubber," the score is "N." Although the concept is not faulty, the multiple delimitation of dimensions makes the sort concretely descriptive of the items placed together rather than conceptual, and an incorrect connotation would be conveyed by giving a score of adequate span. Similarly, when the scoring is extremely concrete (large and toy pliers, called "pliers" or two sugar cubes described, "You eat them"), once again the score is "N" because the whole character of the response is restrictive, even if technically an adequate description.

When a grouping forms a "sub-sort" of a more natural or more obvious basic grouping, the score of "N" is given. For example, when only the toy tools or only the toy silverware are grouped, even if they are accurately described ("toy tools"), the scoring is "N" because of the implication that there is a more basic grouping possible (tools, some toys and some not, or toys, some tools and some not).

Sometimes a patient omits an obvious item from the grouping because he does not notice it rather than because he has a reason for leaving it out. Such omissions are to be recognized as carelessness or a lack of thoroughness, that is, as a possible characterological pattern rather than as a thought process or ego difficulty. Similarly, anxiety or manic erraticness may have an effect on the patient's efficiency and it is important to distinguish this as a secondary level impairment rather than a more basic ego problem. When the examiner feels that the patient's responses do not yield enough data to clarify these points, he can elicit further material. The examiner can probe but should avoid giving directional cues; he may hesitate or look questioningly as if to say, "I wonder if you are aware of your error." This non-verbal behavior generates considerable pressure on the patient to reassess his production and frequently yields important data: can the patient utilize this kind of feedback from the environment? Can he retrace his mental processes? In effect, we test the self-observing and screening functions of the ego. Can the patient, with the induced suspicion that something is wrong, test his use of concept and scan his implementation for flaws? If the non-directive pressure does not appear adequate to help the patient, the examiner can point to an object not included in the grouping and ask whether this item was considered. Here it is recognized that the examiner is extending his own ego to foster better ego functioning on the patient's part. This process elicits additional data regarding how much support is needed before the patient can take advantage of environmental "feedback" and before he himself can recognize defects in his functioning. In these situations, the original response merits a narrow score, but if the patient is able to improve his response, in recording the score, an arrow is added pointing toward the score obtained with added support.

Considerations in scoring "loose." One of the problems encountered is how to score some common sortings that might appear to be fabulations. For example, with the tools, the nails and the block of wood are sorted and explained as "tools and related materials." The score of "1" is given here because there is an obvious communicative relationship. However, if the patient were to add the lock and explain that "it would be used to lock the box in which the tools are kept," the score "(L)" is merited.

Again, the verbal description is critical in evaluation. In one case the bell and the tools placed together and explained as "tools to put the bell on a bike," are scored concrete "(C)" but not loose; however, the bell and tools described as "tools" and left at that, merit "L." The bell here is a gratuitous addition and not given any rationalization, thus raising a suspicion of a flaw in screening, judgment, and ego-reflective capacity. In other words, the patient shows no awareness that his verbal statement does not "fit" the actual grouping.

As in the consideration of narrow span, the examiner may seek data regarding the ability of the patient to reappraise his behavior with some external support. The examiner can communicate that he is wondering if the patient wants to leave the grouping as it is and observe the patient's response. Of course, this added information that implies "something is amiss" may not benefit the patient in gaining closer adherence to reality and he may pursue further tangential associations and make his response even less adequate. It is important to determine whether the patient is aware of the liberty he may be taking in determining the meaning of an item, and the examiner may ask, "Why did you include this?" Observing what appears to be gross looseness, for example, the silverware and a piece of paper called a "place setting," E can ask about the paper. In this example, if the patient says, "Well, it's a piece of paper but I thought it could represent a napkin," he is yielding information about his self-observational capacity when some external support encourages this process. We note that, on his own, he assumes that his thoughts were being communicated and this suggests some weakness in reality appraisal.

Examples of span scores for Part I. In order to illustrate the scoring of span, various sortings for typical concepts are given. Examples for the first item cannot be given, since the sample object is chosen by the patient.

2.   Fork: silverware and/or table setting concept.

N: toy fork or toy fork and large spoon.

(N): large silver only.

n: most of large and small silverware.

+: large knife and spoon, small knife, fork and spoon.

l: none.

(L): silverware with sugar or sink stopper or both, with a fabulation about sugar for coffee or washing the silver in the sink. (Inclusion of the sink stopper and the paper disk is "L".) The degree of looseness implied in such a sorting depends upon the intellectual level of the patient. The same considerations apply to the inclusion of the paper disk as a hot pad.

L: silverware, lock, or tools, or smoking equipment, or ball, in a fabulation.

L: silverware, sugar, sink stopper, paper disc as a table setting and materials related to the kitchen.

3.   Pipe: "smoking" concept.

N: matches, or any one of the other smoking items.

N: cigar and cigarettes, *if* the explanation is in terms of using them to get tobacco for the pipe.

(N): cigar and cigarette, with or without matches.

n: only one imitation item (of cigar or cigarette) or the matches omitted.

4a. Bell: "toy" concept.

N: ball, toy silverware, or toy tools.

(N): toy silverware, toy tools, and ball.

n: sorting minus one or two minor items (e.g., candy cigarette, rubber cigar).

+: ball, toy silverware, toy tools, candy cigarette, rubber cigar.

l: + items with paper forms ("children would play with these, too").

(L): most of + items with large tools ("a child could get into his Dad's tools").

L: all of the items ("someone could play with it all").

4b. Bell: round concept.

N: paper disc, sink stopper.

(N): ball, disc, sink stopper.

(n): one + item omitted.

+: ball, disc, sink stopper, corks, cigarette.

l: pipe added to + items (round bowl).

(L): nails and/or cigar added.

L: everything with some portion being round is included (e.g., screwdrivers or hammer because their handles are round).

5a. Paper disc: round concept.

N: sink stopper only.

(N): sink stopper and ball.

n: one minor item omitted from + listing.

+: ball, sink stopper, corks, cigarette, bell.

l: pipe added to + items (round bowl).

(L): nails and/or cigar added.

L: everything with some portion being round is included (e.g., screwdrivers or hammer because their handles are round).

5b. Paper disc: paper concept.

N: one other paper item.

(N): paper shapes (square and 3 x 5 card).

n: + items with one omission.

+: paper square, 3 x 5 card, cigarette, matchbook.

l: none.

(L): eraser added to + items ("it's a school item").

L: wood block and sugar cubes added ("They have similar shapes").

5c. Paper disc: red concept.

N: rubber ball.

(N): rubber ball, sink stopper.

n: one + item omitted.

+: ball, stopper, matchbook, eraser.

l: + items and red handled screwdriver.

(L): rubber or real cigar added because "band has a touch of red."

L: bell added because "red means danger and bell is also a danger signal."

6. Toy pliers: "tool" concept.

N: large pliers; or any grossly incomplete grouping.

N: block with nail, "to pull the nail out."

(N): toy tools.

n: unsystematic omission, as of toy hatchet only.

+: four miniature tools and two large tools.

l: toy and large tools with nails, wood blocks.

(L): + items with lock added ("to lock tool box").

L: + items (or most of them) with pipe, cigar, or cigarette, "because the worker would smoke while using the tools."

7a. Ball: toy concept.

N: bell or toy silverware or toy tools.

(N): bell, toy silverware, toy tools.

n:, + sorting minus one or two items.

+: bell, toy tools, toy silverware, candy cigarette, rubber cigar.

l: + items with paper forms.

(L): + items and large tools ("could play with them too").

L: all items ("someone could play with all of them").

7b. Ball: rubber concept.

N: sink stopper ("they're round *and* rubber").

(N): one rubber item omitted.

n: none.

+: eraser, sink stopper, cigar.

l: none.

(L): corks added ("they're also a soft material like rubber").

L: add wood as well as corks ("all really come from trees").

Listings of items in groupings in Part II

The items included in each conceptual category are those listed by Holt in the revised *Diagnostic Psychological Testing*. Adjustments would naturally have to be made contingent upon how one builds his Sorting Test kit. For example, if a white candy cigarette is used for the imitation cigarette, this would affect the White and Rubber sorts as presented below.

CONCEPT	ITEMS
1. Red	Ball, paper disk, matchbook, sink stopper, eraser (No partly red items).
2. Metal	Large silverware, small silverware, bell, lock, nails (2), pliers (2)
3. Round	Ball, sink stopper, corks (2), bell, paper disk.
4. Tools	Large and small screwdriver, large and small pliers, hammer, hatchet.
5. Paper	Paper disk, green cardboard square, white filing card, matchbook, real cigarette.
6. Pairs	All items of which there are two, whether real or imitation.
7. White	Real cigarette, sugar cubes (2), filing card, green square turned on its reverse (white) side.

8.	Rubber	Sink stopper, imitation cigar, imitation cigarette (if rubber), ball, eraser.
9.	Smoking	Pipe, real cigar and cigarette, imitation cigar and cigarette, matchbook.
10.	Silverware	Large silverware, small silverware.
11.	Toys	Four small tools, three small eating utensils, imitation cigar, imitation cigarette, ball.
12.	Rectangles	Filing card, green paper, square, block of wood with nail in it, matchbook, sugar cubes (2).

List of items and suggested symbols for use in the Sorting Test [4]

(1)	C	Cigar	(10)[5]	saw	Toy saw
(2)	c	Rubber cigar	(11)	ham	Toy hammer
(3)	Cigt	Cigarette	(12)[6]	◼	Cardboard square (red with white reverse side)
(4)	cigt	Imitation cigarette			
(5)	m	Match folder (red)	(13)	◯	Cardboard disc - red
(6)	Pl	Pliers	(14)	▭	File card - white
(7)	pl	Toy pliers	(15)	lk	Lock
(8)	SD	Screwdriver	(16)	sug	Sugar cubes (2)
(9)	sd	Toy screwdriver	(17)	⊡	Block with nail

[4] These items are listed by Holt in the revised *Diagnostic Psychological Testing* with the few exceptions noted.

[5] In the Rapaport Sorting Test, a toy hatchet was used.

[6] The Rapaport Sorting Test used a green paper square instead of a red one.

(18) SS   Sink stopper (red rubber)

(19) Ba   Ball - red, rubber

(20) Be   Bell

(21) ck   Corks (2)

(22) n   Nails (2)

(23) E   Eraser (red, rubber, rectangular)

(24) K   Knife

(25) F   Fork

(26) S   Spoon

(27) k   Toy knife

(28) f   Toy fork

(29) s   Toy spoon

(30) P   Pipe

REFERENCES

ANASTASI, A., Psychology, psychologists and psychological testing, *American Psychologist,*1967, **22**, 297-306.

BANTA, T. J., Tests for the evaluation of early childhood education: The Cincinnati Autonomy Test Battery, in J. Hellmuth (Ed.), *Cognitive Studies,* Brunner/Mazel, New York, 1970, in press.

COLARELLI, N. J. & SIEGEL, S. M., *Ward H: An Adventure in Innovation,* Van Nostrand, New York, 1966.

CUMMING, J. & CUMMING, E., *Ego and Milieu,* Atherton Press, New York, 1966.

DesLAURIERS, A. M., *The Experience of Reality in Childhood Schizophrenia,* International Universities Press, New York, 1962.

ERIKSON, E., *Childhood and Society,* Norton, New York, 1950.

FEDERN, P., *Ego Psychology and the Psychoses* (Eduardo Weiss, Ed.) Basic Books, New York, 1953.

FREEMAN, T., CAMERON, J., & McGHIE, A., *Chronic Schizophrenia,* International Universities Press, New York, 1958.

FREUD, A., Mutual influences in the development of ego and id, Vol. 7, *Psychoanalytic Study of the Child,* International Universities Press, New York, 1952, pp. 42-50.

FREUD, S., The ego and the id (1923), in J. Rickman (Ed.), *A General Selection from the Works of Sigmund Freud,* Doubleday, New York, 1957, pp. 210-35.

HARTMANN, H., Ego psychology and the problem of adaptation (1939), in D. Rapaport (Ed.), *Organization and Pathology of Thought,* Columbia University Press, New York, 1951, pp. 362-96.

HIRT, M. L. & KAPLAN, M. L., Psychological testing II. Current practice, *Comprehensive Psychiatry,* 1967, **8** (5), 310-20.

HOLLON, T. H., Ego psychology and the supportive therapy of depression and borderline states. Paper presented at a seminar of the Department of Psychiatry, University of Cincinnati College of Medicine, April, 1965.

HOLLON, T. H., Ego psychology and the supportive therapy of borderline states, *Psychotherapy: Theory, Research and Practice,* 1966, **3** (3), 135-8.

HOLT, R. R., The emergence of cognitive psychology, *Journal of the American Psychoanalytic Association,* 1964, **12**, 650-65.

HOLT, R. R., Diagnostic testing: Present status and future prospects, *Journal of Nervous and Mental Disease,* 1967, **144** (6), 444-65.

HOLT, R. R., Revised edition of Rapaport, D., Gill, M., & Schafer, R. *Diagnostic Psychological Testing,* International Universities Press, New York, 1968.

HUNT, J. McV., Traditional personality theory in the light of recent evidence, *American Scientist,* 1965, **53** (No. 1), 80-96.

KAPLAN, M. L., Maintaining continuity of experience in organic deficit, *Journal of Individual Psychology,* 1964, **20**, 48-54.

KAPLAN, M. L., Ego impairment and ego adaptation in schizophrenia, *Journal of Projective Techniques,* 1967, **31**, 7-17.

KAPLAN, M. L., HIRT, M. L., & KURTZ, R. M., Psychological testing: I. History and current trends, *Comprehensive Psychiatry,* 1967, **8** (No. 5), 299-309.

KENISTON, K., *The Uncommitted: Alienated Youth in American Society,* Harcourt, Brace & World, New York, 1965.

KLEIN, G. S., The personal world through perception, in R. R. Blake & G. V. Ramsey (Eds.), *Perception: An Approach to Personality,* Ronald Press, New York, 1951, pp. 328-55.

KNIGHT, R. P., Borderline states, in R. P. Knight & C. Friedman (Eds.), *Psychoanalytic Psychiatry and Psychology,* International Universities Press, New York, 1954, pp. 97-109.

NUNBERG, H., The synthetic function of the ego (1930), in *Practice and Theory of Psychoanalysis,* Nervous and Mental Diseases (Pub.), New York, 1948, pp. 120-36.

RAPAPORT, D., The autonomy of the ego, *Bulletin of the Menninger Clinic,* 1951, **15**, 113-23.

RAPAPORT, D., Toward a theory of thinking, in D. Rapaport (Ed.), *Organization and Pathology of Thought: Selected Sources,* Columbia University Press, New York, 1951, pp. 689-770.

RAPAPORT, D., Projective techniques and the theory of thinking (1952), in M. M. Gill (Ed.), *The Collected Papers of David Rapaport,* Basic Books, New York, 1967, pp. 461-9.

RAPAPORT, D., GILL, M., & SCHAFER, R., *Diagnostic Psychological Testing,* Vol. I, Year Book, Chicago, 1945.

SCHACTEL, E. G., Subjective definitions of the Rorschach test situation and their effect on test performance, *Psychiatry,* 1943, **6**, 393-409.

SCHAFER, R., Psychological tests in clinical research, *Journal of Consulting Psychology,* 1949, **13**, 328-34.

SCHAFER, R., *Psychoanalytic Interpretation in Rorschach Testing,* Grune & Stratton, New York, 1954.

WHITE, R. W., Motivation reconsidered: The concept of competence, *Psychological Review,* 1959, **66**, 297-333.

DATE DUE

MAR 01 '92			
MAR 20 '92			
GAYLORD			PRINTED IN U.S.A.